Existential Science Fiction

Existential Science Fiction

Ryan Lizardi

LEXINGTON BOOKS
Lanham • Boulder • New York • London

Published by Lexington Books
An imprint of The Rowman & Littlefield Publishing Group, Inc.
4501 Forbes Boulevard, Suite 200, Lanham, Maryland 20706
www.rowman.com

86-90 Paul Street, London EC2A 4NE, United Kingdom

Copyright © 2022 by The Rowman & Littlefield Publishing Group, Inc.

All rights reserved. No part of this book may be reproduced in any form or by any electronic or mechanical means, including information storage and retrieval systems, without written permission from the publisher, except by a reviewer who may quote passages in a review.

British Library Cataloguing in Publication Information Available

Library of Congress Cataloging-in-Publication Data

Names: Lizardi, Ryan, 1981- author.
Title: Existential science fiction / Ryan Lizardi.
Description: Lanham : Lexington Books, [2022] | Includes bibliographical references and index. | Summary: "This book explores contemporary existential science fiction media and their influence on society's conceptions of humanity. These media texts manifest abstract concepts in a genre that has historically focused on exploring new ideas and frontiers, creating powerful media that helps audiences contemplate their existence as human beings"—Provided by publisher.
Identifiers: LCCN 2021048391 (print) | LCCN 2021048392 (ebook) |
  ISBN 9781793647351 (cloth) | ISBN 9781793647368 (epub)
Subjects: LCSH: Science fiction films—History and criticism. | Science fiction television programs—History and criticism. | Science fiction—Philosophy. | Existentialism in motion pictures. | Humanism in motion pictures. | Self in motion pictures.
Classification: LCC PN1995.9.S26 L59 2022 (print) | LCC PN1995.9.S26 (ebook) |
  DDC 791.43/615—dc23/eng/20211004
LC record available at https://lccn.loc.gov/2021048391
LC ebook record available at https://lccn.loc.gov/2021048392

∞^{TM} The paper used in this publication meets the minimum requirements of American National Standard for Information Sciences—Permanence of Paper for Printed Library Materials, ANSI/NISO Z39.48-1992.

Contents

Preface vii

1 Early Existential Science Fiction 1
2 Modern Existential Science Fiction 15
3 *Gravity*, *Ad Astra*, and Generational Connections 35
4 *Interstellar*, *Arrival*, and Continuity of Identity 49
5 *Annihilation* and Refraction of Identity 63
6 *Legion* and Fractured Identity 79
7 *Westworld* and the Embellished Remake 93
8 *Assassin's Creed*, *Bioshock*, and Alternative Histories 111
9 Interactive Existential Science Fiction 129

Concluding Remarks 143
Bibliography 147
Index 155
About the Author 157

Preface

Hollywood blockbusters with no clear human (or alien) antagonists, slow-paced video games that redefine interactivity at a granular level, and deep introspection and contemplation of self at every mediated turn. These characteristics do not immediately come to mind when thinking about the science fiction genre, which is more prone to starcruiser battles with laser cannons and world-dominating alien invasions. This book explores contemporary existential science fiction media (films, television, and video games) and their influence on our conceptions of memory, identity, and humanity. Specifically, the ways in which a recent cluster of science fiction media such as the films *Gravity* (2013), *Interstellar* (2014), *Arrival* (2016), *Annihilation* (2018), and *Ad Astra* (2019); television shows like *Legion* (2017–2019) and *Westworld* (2016–present); and video games like *SOMA* (2015) and *Death Stranding* (2019) present a vision of the future that is inextricably tied to a version of self that is more contemplative and comparative than traditional science fiction media. What is it about our current cultural landscape that fosters content dealing directly with questions about our identity, our memory, and our continuity of self, but does so through the setting of science fiction and space exploration? These works seem to be leveraging the external trappings of the science fiction genre, often through space exploration, to explore internal thematic ideas of reaching without and within ourselves to find a continuity of our individual and collective identities.

To pretend that a genre of fiction that uses as a backdrop the pushing of the limits of where human beings can possibly go as well as what they can possibly achieve and invent is only newly existential is wrong. Many historical works have dealt with the intersection of science fiction, existential longing, and identity formation, such as *Blade Runner* (1982) and *Contact* (1997). There are also plenty of contemporary science fiction media that are not overtly existential in nature, such as the *Star Wars* sequel trilogy (2015–2019) with its clear focus on action or even *The Martian* (2015) that has many of the trappings of existential science fiction without the actual existential questions posed. So instead of assuming a new mantle of existentialism, this book works from the premise that though tendencies toward existential thought and musings were always an inherent part of the science fiction genre, a cluster of recent works in film, television, and video games have further leveraged philosophical thought as a way to provide a potentially more healthy and contemplative lens through which to view our existence as human beings. The current wave of existential science fiction narrative thematic content has leaned into a contemplative pose, potentially signaling that audiences and media industries alike are now more hospitable toward consistent philosophical musings alongside space exploration and scientific speculation. The time is right for an alternative formation of science fiction based more on explorations of human existence and identity formation.

SOME DEFINITIONS AND HEURISTICS

There is an important distinction between existential and existentialism. There is a reason this book is not called "Existentialism in Science Fiction." This book will certainly engage with the philosophy of existentialism when applicable, with plenty of Sartre throughout, but the methodology of this book will be much broader. The argument of this book is that to explore the existential is to look at all that it means to exist as a human being. Questions about who we are, where we have been and are going, and the why of it all are just as important as the classic existentialism questions about essence, absurdity, and authenticity. This means that there will be science fiction media discussed in these chapters that speak more to a humanism philosophy of existence, media that will be shown to engage in a strictly rational scientific inquiry into existence, some that introduce religious thematics into the world of science fiction, and other media that is undoubtedly existentialist. Regardless of the strict historical philosophical definitions, this book will take the broader view that the contemporary cultural cluster of existential science fiction media is contemplative about our identity, our memory, and our continuity of self as human beings.

Antagonists, or a lack thereof, play an interesting role in existential science fiction media, as they often stand counterposed to media in the same genre that present more explicit villains, human or otherwise. One heuristic to apply is whether the central focus of a given existential media text is more concerned with asking questions about human existence than in defeating some kind of villainous force. Existential science fiction media are not devoid of drama or action, but this heuristic would be about what the media's primary focus is. For instance, a film like *The Core* (2003), about the Earth's core inexplicably ceasing to rotate and a mission to restart it with an explosion, resembles more contemporary science fiction film plots like *Sunshine* (2007), but emphasizes action-heavy sequences far above any form of existential thematics. So plotting on a four quadrant graph of sorts, with the x-axis being level of existential exploration and the y-axis being level of action/antagonist, a film like *The Core* would likely occupy the upper left quadrant, while a film like *Arrival* would be situated in the bottom right. I struggle to identify what science fiction film would occupy the bottom left quadrant, hypothetically being devoid of both action/antagonists and existential thought, but a film series like *Star Wars* might occupy the upper right quadrant. The *Star Wars* franchise is not devoid of existential thought, as its musing of the "force" and its binding power in the universe has elements of this philosophical inquiry; however, the primary focus appears to be lightsaber battles with foes from the dark side of the force. There is no Darth Vader in *Arrival*. When a character named Dr. Brand from *Interstellar* talks villains with the main character Cooper, she says that in space "we face great odds, death, but not evil." There still must be drama, but instead of sinister bad guys, so many existential science fiction media rely on forces of science and nature to provide dramatic intrigue. Cooper responds by asking Dr. Brand, "You don't think nature can be evil?" to which she answers, "Formidable, frightening, but no, not evil." Sure there's a stray human here and there that provides momentary obstacles for protagonists in these existential science fiction media, such as the selfish Dr. Mann in *Interstellar* or the scared troops with a bomb in *Arrival*, but the main focus is on the thematic inquiry into our humanity. Applying this heuristic is also not the only criteria, as a film like *The Martian* has no true antagonist, aside from the literal inhospitable environment of Mars, but the film itself is not overtly existential. So it checks one box, but not another. On the flip side, a film like *Ex Machina* is undoubtedly existentially focused, as it uses a plot about artificially intelligent androids to work through primary themes surrounding ideas of humanity, identity, and consciousness, but distinctly has an ambiguously villainous antagonist in the form of the android creator, Nathan Bateman.

Another important distinction that will be made throughout this book is whether a given existential science fiction media text wound up being influential and inspired other similar works within the same medium and time period. Identifying the trendsetters in the trends can provide insight into what types of stories, genres, and narrative structures are valued by audiences and industries at a given time. So, for instance, *Contact* is a 1997 film that checks a lot of the discussed existential science fiction heuristic boxes, such as its lack of a true antagonist and its clear engagement with existential themes and questions. It is a film about the question of whether we are alone in the universe, and has its main character asking questions like "What are we doing here? Who are we?" When the main character is presented with the opportunity to potentially sacrifice her life to find the answers, she says, "If this is a chance to find out even just a little part of that answer, I don't know, I think it's worth a human life. Don't you?" The difference between a film like *Contact* and a film like *Gravity* is that the science fiction films that followed the former did not resemble it as much as the ones that followed the latter.

So if it is true that over the past decade or so the trend has moved toward the more contemplative science fiction media text, it begs the question of why has a constellation of science fiction works that have been produced recently been more explicit in their connection to philosophical ideas about the human condition? Many of my scholarly works have previously explored these kinds of cultural clusters, where cultural artifacts are separately produced across media but seem to be speaking in conversation with each other about a given topic. For instance, I have previously explored cultural clusters of zombie media in the first decade of the twenty-first century, and have looked at a cluster of alien invasion video games within a five-year period, that all dealt explicitly with issues of ideological othering. I have also previously published three books (two solo-authored, one edited) about the idea of the cultural cluster of nostalgic texts currently dominating contemporary media. This book will simply extend this methodology of exploring the formation and trajectory of cultural clusters to contemporary existential science fiction media.

BRIEF CHAPTERS OVERVIEW

Determining how this contemporary cluster functions, it will be important to lay the historical groundwork that led to this point. The first two chapters of this book will deal with the historical nature of the science fiction genre and its existential musings across media. Neither of these chapters will be intended to imply that questions of humanity and existence are solely a newer phenomenon, quite the contrary. Instead, the historical trajectory of science fiction will be explored for the ways in which existential themes developed, stalled, shifted, or flourished given certain parameters of different time periods and media. The first chapter in this section will explore early existential science fiction, and roughly cover science fiction's media beginnings through the 1950s and the explosion of science fiction during this era. There will be a significant imbalance in focus on science fiction television and film in this early era, given not only my research expertise on these subjects relative to literature but also because of the focus of the rest of the book on more contemporary existential science fiction media. Special attention will be paid to historical works that dealt with the intersection of science fiction, existential longing, and identity formation, with films such as *A Trip to the Moon* (1902), *Metropolis* (1927), *Frankenstein* (1931), and *Destination Moon* (1950) playing significant roles. The next chapter will extend this historical exploration from the 1960s through the early 2000s in an attempt to delineate the differences in how questions of humanity and existence shifted significantly through these time periods, mirroring broader media trends. This chapter will look deeply at *2001: A Space Odyssey* (1968), *Solaris* (1972), and *Blade Runner* (1982) as three films that contain deep philosophical content, but perhaps failed to inspire this trend broadly during the historical time periods that immediately followed. I will then look to turn-of-the-century films like *A.I.: Artificial Intelligence* (2001) and *Prometheus* (2012) to highlight nascent existential science fiction trend line characteristics that would become prominent over the past decade or so. The third chapter then looks to the bookends of the current existential science fiction trend, positioning *Gravity* as the fully realized beginning and *Ad Astra* (2019) as the most recent prominent example. Both films share science fiction DNA in their space travel settings and share thematic elements of generational connections and the definition of existence, which works as a powerful existential combination.

The next section of this book will shift focus to the idea of identity and how contemporary existential science fiction is uniquely positioned to "enable sense-making in relation to the precariousness of life and the basics of 'why are we here'" (Lagerkvist 2017, 98). This section follows the theme of identity through different versions of who we are and how we could come to actualize our identity. In chapter 4, the focus is on two films, *Interstellar* (2014) and *Arrival* (2016), that work through the continuity, and sometimes cyclical nature, of our identities. Both of these films use memories and interstellar space travelers as a foundation for this existential inquiry. The next chapter looks at refracted identity and does so through a deep exploration of the book *Annihilation* (2014) compared to its 2018 film adaptation. Medium differences are examined for the ways in which the versions of the text do, and do not, contain the same forms of existential identity exploration. The next chapter looks at the science fiction television series *Legion* (2017–2019) for the ways in which it depicts identity and its continuity as fractured. This surrealist series deals with mental illness, memory, time, and existence itself, all wrapped in the traditionally safe commercial space of the superhero story. By working through these three versions of identity exploration, continuity, refraction, and fracture, this section argues for the richness of contemporary existential science fiction.

The next section of the book shifts to a focus on medium as a significant way in which existential science fiction explores questions of who we are. In chapter 7, I look at remakes and the differences between existential science fiction across historical eras and film/television media through the contrasting of the *Westworld* (1973) film and the television series remake. The next chapter looks at two modern existential science fiction video game series, *Bioshock* (2007–2013) and *Assassin's Creed* (2007–present), as examples of interactive texts that take accepted histories and challenge their assumptions and inevitability through counterfactual and apocryphal interactive historical representations. The interactive existential combination critique continues in the final chapter of the book, with a look at the ways in which challenges to player expectations and meta-commentaries can leverage the video game medium into a particularly strong philosophical experience. I primary explore *SOMA* (2015) and *Death Stranding* (2019) for their unique destabilizing gameplay and existential narrative content. Combine the digital existential nature with the science fiction genre, with its ability to manifest these abstract concepts in a generic environment historically about the exploration of new frontiers and ideas, and you get a powerful pair of video games that ask their players to contemplate what it means to exist, think, and connect as human beings. At the conclusion of this chapter, it is hoped that when taking all of these media clusters into account, I will have successfully presented the argument that the contemporary media environment has become hospitable to a level of existential thematic content that might not have been possible, or well-received, in earlier time periods.

One thing is clear, which is any number of other media scholars could take the subject of existential science fiction into a multitude of other directions, exploring different media texts along the way. This speaks to the level of further research that could be performed on the subject but also on the ways this book is a particular representative constellation of media texts, but not nearly the comprehensive whole of the subgenre. As is often the case when I write books, I find there are films, television shows, and video games that warrant exploration but do not fit into a given chapter or section theme. It is a weighting of sorts, as the two historical chapters each cover roughly fifty years of science fiction media content and the lion's share of the rest of the book covers ten years, from 2010 to present. Any researcher who was so inclined could write an exploration of existential science fiction media and flip this imbalanced script. If readers found that flip to be more appropriate, I embrace that criticism of my particular subjective perspective, and welcome subsequent research to rectify this perceived imbalance.

Chapter 1

Early Existential Science Fiction

One of the most important points that I hope this book gets across is that the contemporary shift to existential thought in the science fiction genre was gradual, as opposed to a sudden addition of this focus. There is a deep history in science fiction of existential musings about who we are as human beings, how we came to be who we are, and where we are headed in the future. If your interest in reading this book lies solely in exploring recent science fiction films like *Interstellar* and video games like *Death Stranding*, I suppose you could feel free to skip the next two chapters that focus on the existential science fiction historical time line, but I sincerely hope you stick with this long lead-up as it is so important to fully understand contemporary existential science fiction. More specifically, this historical trajectory will be shown to move from often action-based and sometimes allegorical early science fiction to the current cluster of science fiction media that directly takes on existential exploration, and longingly explores the connections between who we are as humans.

Most of the attention of this book will focus on science fiction audiovisual media texts, not because the literature is not important, but because the end goal is to fully engage the contemporary cultural cluster of existential science fiction media texts. Science fiction literature not only has a deep history of existential themes and thought but also has historically used philosophical thought as foundational to the literary genre, with many works far outpacing other science fiction media in their overt focus on questions of humanity and our existence. Books like *The History of Science Fiction* (2016) by Adam Roberts and *Science Fiction: A Literary History* (2017) edited by Roger Luckhurst provide a much more comprehensive exploration of the history of science fiction literature for readers who are interested. The issue is not science fiction literature's lack of existential thematic significance, but more so the lack of available space in a book such as this to fully engage with the genre in the written medium. Science fiction literature is, however, inextricable from the overall genre and its development, and will be addressed when connections can be made to its influence on science fiction media. Not only does much of the audiovisual science fiction media derive its source material from science fiction literature, but this foundational genre outlet also provides unparalleled avenues for genre experimentation and introspection that are not as often afforded within the media and commercial confines of film, television, and video games. However, once film, and later television, began consistently making science fiction content, the connection between audiovisual and literature became more symbiotic than unidirectional. Bradley Schauer describes this "interrelationship and mutual influence of the film industry and American popular culture, as they help to shape the status of the SF genre" (2016, 5). Schauer argues that the genre elasticity is influenced by everything from the culture the genre is being made within to media of the genre to the popular discussion and the fandom surrounding the genre.

Crucial for this book is that within this idea of genre elasticity is the ability for the science fiction genre to take the kernel of its essence (the exploration of who we are, where we are headed, and how we fit within the universe), and seek out hospitable production, commercial, and reception environments to fully embody this essence. Many genre theorists work from similar foundations of genre definitions, seeking to account for many factors in what does and does not count in a given categorization. For instance, Rick Altman is one of the most prominent film genre theorists, and developed a distinction that is of particular importance to this book's arguments. Altman describes the difference between "semantic" genre elements that are "common traits, attitudes, characters, shots, locations, sets" that make up a "genre's building blocks," and "syntactic . . . constitutive relationships" in a genre that "privileges the structures into which they are arranged" (1984, 10). On one side, the semantic, we have the recognizable things that identify to audiences that they are watching a given genre, and on the other side, the syntactic, we have the thematic material and structures commonly found in a genre. So for the purposes of this book, Altman's distinction will be used as a methodological heuristic to determine whether a given media text readily fits within accepted science fiction genre definitions, using semantic elements (and some syntactic), and whether said media text is existential in nature, using syntactic constitutive relationships. By doing so, it will be evident that existential themes in science fiction books, films, and television shows exist at the very beginnings of the genre itself, which will be explored in this chapter, but it is not until later when certain commercial restraints are alleviated that existential inquiry can flourish.

This changing nature of the definition of the science fiction genre will be of huge importance for this chapter, but equally important will be to understand the way this genre fluidity stems from the many cultural, historical, and industrial factors that arise during a given era. Schauer argues this point in saying that a "definition of SF rooted in both industrial discourse and production cycles avoids ahistorical, essentialist models and recognizes that genre is a fluid, historically contingent construct" (2016, 7). As such, the use of a methodological approach that engages with industry and commercial factors that directly influence the type of science fiction content made across given time periods seems appropriate. Schauer makes the reasons for these changes explicit saying that as researchers we should be "connecting cultural contexts to industrial and economic determinants, to reveal how these have interwoven to shape the development of the SF film genre in America" (2016, 4). Important for this book, and this chapter, as it deals with existential trends in science fiction media across time, Schauer describes how in science fiction,

> depending on the historical period, different strategies have risen to prominence, including an emphasis on scientific accuracy, the use of art cinema style and narration, political content, spectacular special effects, greater psychological complexity and nuanced characterization, the involvement of major stars, the guidance of an auteur director, the avoidance of camp, and fantasy world-building through production design. (2016, 8)

The reasons for these strategy changes would certainly be culturally influenced, as well as influenced by the technological capabilities of a given time period, but what was considered most economically viable would have been of great concern for companies making science fiction media. This would align the methodology of this chapter, and book at large, with critical media industrial perspectives that

> examine the relationships between strategies (here read as the larger economic goals and logics of large-scale cultural industries) and tactics (the ways in which cultural workers seek to negotiate, and at times perhaps subvert, the constraints imposed by institutional interests to their own purposes). (Havens et al. 2009, 247)

This seems to be an appropriate bridge, given the way the study of how "institutional discourses are internalized and acted upon by cultural workers" is argued to be the "missing link between political economy's concentration on larger economic structural forces and much of cultural studies' analyses of end products such as media texts and audience interpretations" (Havens et al. 2009, 247). So exploring how a given media industry's receptiveness, or lack thereof in the case of the media explored here, to complex existential questions in science fiction during a given historical era will be the primary focus of this chapter.

EARLY SCIENCE FICTION FILMS

The amount of influence and history behind the science fiction genre and its transition to audiovisual media like film and television is varied and vast, and would not serve the purposes of this book to explore comprehensively. Instead, this section will look to a few key examples of science fiction films released during the beginning decades of the medium. This structure will lead to a more in-depth discussion of 1950s science fiction films, given that some have argued that this is "when SF was first recognized by the industry as a distinct genre" (Schauer 2016, 4). Beginning with silent science fiction films *A Trip to the Moon* (1902) and *Metropolis* (1927), then moving to the ambiguous genre film *Frankenstein* (1931), and finally to serials *Flash Gordon* (1936) and *King of the Rocket Men* (1949), this section will present early science fiction media as primarily focused on the action-based antagonism of the genre and not on the existential potentials contained therein.

When Georges Méliès released *A Trip to the Moon* in 1902, it was a big success and has been historically recognized as one of the most influential films of all time, in many ways launching a rocket and a genre all at once. However, it was not the existentially focused version of science fiction that the genre has grown to become. Partially due to the practical limitations of the medium in its early form, there is not much depth to any exploration of our existential relationship with the universe in this fictional film about humans' first space travel. There is only so much that can be done in twelve minutes. However, being that many regard *A Trip to the Moon* as the first science fiction film, there are nascent elements of these themes, such as the desire of man to push the boundaries of science and the relationship to those that might exist not on Earth. The inspiration for this influential film is complicated, despite the certainty of director Georges Méliès who said that the idea "came to me from the book[s] of Jules Verne, entitled 'From the earth to the moon and round the moon' [*sic*]. In this work the human people could not attain the moon" so he "imagined, in using the process of Jules Verne, (gun and shell) to attain the moon" (Lefebvre 2011, 50). In fact, Thierry Lefebvre notes clear inspirations outside of this book, from fairground lectures to operas to other books and films, saying that "*A Trip to the Moon* is a heterogenous film. Taken from a patchwork of sources, which are probably more complex and varied than Méliès made out to be the case" (2011, 53). Furthermore, this patchwork of ideas is used as a way for Méliès to utilize all of the cinematic tricks and fantastical techniques that he would become famous for mastering, as opposed to providing some kind of deep existential commentary. Méliès notes that "the scenario so executed was of no importance whatsoever because my sole aim was to use it as a 'pretext' for the 'staging,' for the 'tricks,' or for picturesque tableaux" (Gauderault 1987, 114). Discussing this quote, David Sandner argues that the

> central idea of *A Trip to the Moon*, if Méliès is to be believed, is a poetic tableau that includes elements of a fantastic nature that have little or nothing to do with the scientific posturing of Verne or the tightly constructed social parable of Wells. (1998, 17)

Containing many of the elements that turn out to be important throughout the science fiction genre to this day, *Metropolis* (1927) stands as influential to android science fiction stories, dystopian stories, as well as the scientific overreacher plot discussed at length later in this chapter. *Metropolis* contains a great deal of historical commentary on class relations too. The loss of humanity in an oppressive factory environment is evident from the very first shot of human beings in Metropolis, as workers are shown lining up in front of a rising gate for a shift change and walk in a uniform, robotic, and defeated manner. Shoulders slumped, often shot from behind rows of workers, you can see the strained rounded backs of these factory workers and the loss of their individual humanity in the process. This setup is primarily in place to level a critique of the class struggles and a dichotomy between the worker and owner classes. And this struggle is made semantically science fiction, through the leader of the city of Metropolis, Joh Frederson, encouraging the creation of a robot that will be able to embody the leader of a worker uprising, Maria, to trick the revolters into being disillusioned with her. Rotwang, the robot's inventor, tells him that "no man, Joh Frederson, will be able to differentiate the Machine-Man from a mortal," speaking to the early nascent science fiction existential equivalency of humans and other conscious entities.

Heart and its connection to humanity is the most prevalent syntactic thematic device used in *Metropolis*: from the often said mantra of the needed "mediator" between the head and the hands to the transfer of Maria's appearance to the Man-Machine shown as taking hold only when the heart starts beating. The Man-Machine becomes her, not when her brain is transferred, but when her glowing heart is. There are some connections that become obscured in the translation, as Joh tells the robot to go into the depths and destroy "deines vorbildes," which translates to "your role model" or in the Blu-ray version, "your prototype." Then, when discussing the robot with Maria, Joh calls it "Dein Ebenbild," which translates to "your likeness" or in the Blu-ray version, "your clone." These semantic differences do not blunt any form of existential critique of humans versus robotic conscious entities, but they do make their intentions harder to discern and replicate in terms of a trend within the genre.

Horror and science fiction films are obviously not a perfect circle Venn diagram; however, there are important connections that can be made when the horrific elements are based on fantastical scientific creations that take on monstrous characteristics. Even if this were not generally the case, the novel *Frankenstein* (1818) by Mary Shelley represents proto versions of both horror and science fiction, so its adaptation in 1931 is worth exploring for its existential content, even if the sequels and character spin-offs are not worth discussing in this regard. *Frankenstein* opens in a manner befitting its groundbreaking nature, with one of the actors, Edward Van Sloan, breaking the fourth wall and addressing the audience about the shocking and horrifying things they are about to see. A publicity move, to be sure, but it provides the opportunity to directly hear what the filmmakers felt *Frankenstein* was actually about, as Van Sloan describes Dr. Frankenstein as a "man of science who sought to create a man after his own image without reckoning upon God. It is one of the strangest tales ever told. It deals with the two great mysteries of creation; life and death." The film itself does not dwell on these thematic elements too much, though some sequences early in *Frankenstein* do involve Dr. Frankenstein's mentor, Dr. Waldman, who tries to explain Frankenstein's motivations for wanting to create life. The moment Dr. Frankenstein is successful in animating the reconstituted corpse, he utters the often parodied line, "It's alive!," but follows it up with the most explicitly existential line in the whole film, "Now I know what it feels like to be God." *Frankenstein* contained thematic elements surrounding the creation of life and humanity's place in that creation, and given the film's influences on two film genres, horror and science fiction, it could be assumed this syntactic trait would be carried forward. However, given the development of these genres and the trajectory of the character of Frankenstein's monster into schlocky parody, this potential was not fully realized.

Schauer, discussing the various *Flash Gordon*, *Buck Rogers*, and *Superman* serials of the 1930s, argues that the "proliferation of these comic book characters throughout the mass media only served to further perpetuate the common perception of SF as a children's genre, as their appearances in film and radio were, like comic books, clearly aimed at younger audiences" (2016, 25). It is obvious, given these industrial, historical, audience, and genre factors, that science fiction serials like *Flash Gordon* (1936) did not explore complicated existential themes, but instead focused almost exclusively on fantastical and antagonistic-driven plots about space aliens. When guards serving Emperor Ming on the planet Mongo apprehend Flash Gordon, Dr. Alexis Zarkov, and Dale Arden they appear to look and talk just like humans, but this is a product of the science fiction serial genre's budgetary constraints and not a commentary on humanity's equivalence to extraterrestrials. *Flash Gordon* and other serials' successes led to more content of the same type, creating, in some ways, a reverse existential trend within the science fiction genre. Schauer argues this point by saying that "Universal's 1936 *Flash Gordon* serial was expensive for its time and well-received but also contributed to the dominance of the juvenile pulp SF paradigm, to the exclusion of other forms of the genre" (2016, 27). Schauer discussing early 1940s space opera science says, "Critics took issue with space opera's lack of interest in scientific accuracy, its shameless use of convenient pseudoscience . . . and its emphasis on action over philosophical argumentation, political commentary, or informed technological speculation" (2016, 22). The serial science fiction films of the 1940s did not progress much in this regard either, as looking at one of the last entries before the calendar turned to 1950, *King of the Rocket Men* (1949), not much difference can be gleaned. The serial begins with a series of villainous acts by a shadowy man, named Dr. Vulcan, and despite a plethora of scenes that discuss a man wearing a rocket-powered suit, there is nary a hint of depth beyond one scientist calling the endeavor "mad dreams of developing flying suits to change men into human rockets." Not exactly a complex exploration of pioneering science. Instead, *King of the Rocket Men* is primarily concerned with scenes of flying, battles with Dr. Vulcan, and ends in a hail of bombs, putting the serial in line with other science fiction film content of the era. Not much would change throughout the next decade on the big screen, as will be evident looking at the films of the 1950s. And it was not just film where this action over complexity trend continued as Schauer argues that "of all the mass media, it was television that most solidified SF's reputation as cheap and childish in the 1950s" (2016, 28).

1950S SCIENCE FICTION FILM

The shift in decades is important, at the very least as a codifying effect on the film genre, as it was not until "1950, when SF was first recognized by the industry as a distinct genre" (2016, 4). In the late 1940s and early 1950s, "SF was growing increasingly prominent in American culture owing to rising interest in SF literature, rocketry, atomic energy, and the ufo phenomenon. However, the genre was still widely understood to be frivolous and juvenile" (Schauer 2016, 8). The conditions were ripe for the genre to make the full jump to film, but what kind of science fiction would thrive in the Hollywood industrial environment? Though this section will primarily be about 1950s science fiction film, we can use television of the same era and genre as a microcosm of the trajectory of quality/complexity.

Schauer describes how early serialized science fiction television like *Out There* (1951–1952) and *Tales of Tomorrow* (1951–1953) "used reputable Hollywood personnel and were examples of outstanding craftsmanship (within the limitations of early live television) and thoughtful storytelling that would influence later, more successful anthology series like *The Twilight Zone*" (2016, 28). What will be true for film was true for television though, with the allure of the cheap knockoff winning over complicated high-budget content. Schauer describes that "despite the quality of these programs, they were both short-lived and utterly overwhelmed by the large number of juvenile SF shows that illuminated American television screens in the early-to-mid-1950s—none more popular than *Captain Video*" (2016, 28). Schauer argues for a similar trajectory with early SF films, such as *Destination Moon* (1950), which emphasized "scientific realism as a means of legitimation" but this production "mode was soon corrupted as studios began to emphasize more sensational SF story lines" (2016, 8). To explore this shift, it will be helpful to look at some of the key films for the way their semantic and syntactic content developed and shifted along this continuum of realism and sensationalism. This is not to say that realism automatically equals existential depth, or that sensationalism precludes it altogether, but there is a relationship between the two that pulls the focus either toward or away from questions of humanity and our existence.

There is no doubt that *Destination Moon* is not the first science fiction film, with antecedents from Méliès to *Metropolis* to *Flash Gordan* and *Buck Rogers* (1939), but considering its era and influence it is important to examine for its semantic genre elements and its syntactic existential characteristics. In terms of science fiction genre semantics, everything in *Destination Moon* appears fully formed, from space exploration to futuristic technologies and applications. There is a heavy reliance on verisimilitude and science over action and otherworldly antagonists, resembling, in this regard, many contemporary existential science fiction media texts like *Gravity* (2012) and *Interstellar* (2014). *Destination Moon* literally takes the effort to explain the science and physics behind the trip to the moon and back through an intercut Woody Woodpecker cartoon. Relatedly, another 1950 film, *Rocketship X-M*, rushed into production to piggyback off of the release of *Destination Moon*, began as similar in its initial scientific tone but "after its first forty minutes *X-M* departs wildly from the attempted scientific realism of *Destination Moon* and positions itself firmly within the pulp science-fiction tradition" (Schauer 2015, 17). Syntactically, *Destination Moon* does not ask many existential questions beyond a persistent theme of human curiosity and drive, but those elements are certainly present. When investors in the project ask why they should want to build a rocket to the moon, aircraft manufacturer Jim Barnes says that he wants to "because it's never been done, because I don't know." Barnes calls the moon "another north pole" and the trip "pioneering," with media scholar Catherine L. Newell arguing that "with the premier of *Destination Moon*, science fiction finally found a way out of the same old Buck Rogers loop and entered mainstream cinema by utilizing the myth of the American frontier" (2014, 478). This pioneering theme is coupled with overt connections made to the military-industrial complex, with Barnes saying that "only American industry can do this job" and General Thayer remarking that the "first country that can use the moon for the launching of missiles, will control the Earth. That, gentlemen, is the most important military fact of this century." Both statements portend the existing and intensifying space race dynamics, as Newell describes *Destination Moon* capturing the "post-War, pro-industrial capitalism zeitgeist that was fueling America" (2014, 476). When they reach the moon, Dr. Charles Cargraves marks the occasion by saying, "By the grace of God and the name of the United States of America, I take possession of this planet on behalf of and for the benefit of all mankind." Despite this heavy-handed colonial statement, *Destination Moon* is primarily about the science behind the journey, with the last sequence dedicated to intricate weight-to-fuel calculations, presenting a view of space travel quite different from prior filmic representations. From magnetic boots to space walks, the form of science fiction present in this early 1950s film could have become commonplace, and there were others that followed suit. However, Schauer argues this was not the norm going forward, because "by the late 1950s, SF was associated almost exclusively with cheap, culturally disreputable horror films" (2016, 8).

Tracking this shift from complex and potentially contemplative to more shallow and sensational, economic, industrial, and cultural factors all played a part in going from *Destination Moon* to *Plan 9 from Outer Space* (1959). Schauer describes studios' early attempt at the "creation of expansive, believable science fictional environments was tied to the SF A film's primary strategy of differentiation" from pulp influences (2016, 54). This is not to say that there is a direct correlation between high-budget science fiction films versus low-budget ones and their capacity toward existential content, but Schauer makes the connection between the A and B distinction and the complexity contained within a given film. Some early 1950s films tow this line, such as *The Day the Earth Stood Still* (1951), *When Worlds Collide* (1951), and *The War of the Worlds* (1953), but there were exceptions like *The Thing from Another World* (1951) that "unabashedly embraced the genre's most lurid qualities" (2016, 63). Schauer posits a simple economic math equation to explain the shift away from higher-budget science fiction films saying that "while the sf A films of the early-to-mid-1950s were modest successes, most failed to justify their substantial production costs" (2016, 66). This production budget versus box office receipts discrepancy consistently repeated itself, and so "by 1957 the majors had largely relinquished the SF genre to low-budget exploitation producers. The appeal of exploitation films was rooted in their ability to generate a disproportionately large amount of revenue from their tiny budgets" (2016, 78). It is also important to note the obvious connection between the move away from scientifically driven space exploration of the early decade to the monstrous and the fear of atomic nuclear proliferation. M. Keith Booker argues that with "the Cold War political climate of the long 1950s, it is not surprising that many of the most important science fiction works of the decade dealt with the possibility of nuclear holocaust and its aftermath" (2001, 65). Perhaps, first a list of just a few of these films that fall into this mode of production and generic structure would be more helpful to get a sense of their ubiquity. Not close to comprehensive, a few of these films include *It Came from Outer Space* (1953), *The Beast with a Million Eyes* (1955), *Creature with the Atom Brain* (1955), *20 Million Miles to Earth* (1957), *Attack of the Crab Monsters* (1957), *Attack of the 50 Foot Woman* (1958), and *Invisible Invaders* (1959). Given this broad shift to low-budget atomic mutations and alien invasions across the course of the decade, it seems less fruitful to explore in great detail the ways in which each science fiction exploitation film of the 1950s did not tend to prioritize existential exploration over sensationalized action and antagonism. However, exploring just a few exemplary films for the ways in which they broadly functioned as vehicles for fantastic mutations and alien invasions could still be helpful to understanding the phenomenon.

Them! (1954) is about giant ants attacking a desert area in New Mexico, and contains all the hallmarks of this era's science fiction films. Dr. Harold Medford explains that the ants are a "fantastic mutation, probably caused by the lingering radiation from the first atomic bomb," though there is a brief scene where the flying queen ants are not coincidentally described as alien flying saucers. There is definitely budgetary skimping, with off-screen ants announcing themselves with a high-pitched oscillating sound, to avoid having to show them as often, with the first ant not appearing on screen until twenty-eight minutes into the film. The latter half of *Them!* even becomes an odd version of a detective story where an FBI agent, a local cop, and a myrmecologist search for unseen queen ants to save on the budget. The film contains sensational action, but it is a far cry from the theatrical poster that advertised hordes of horrific ants, and shows a level of fiery destruction not present in the film. Schauer calls this the "pulp paradox" and explains how common it was for "sensational qualities of SF A films" to be "exaggerated in their promotional campaigns" leading to potential disappointment while also tagging the film as cheap exploitation in the process (2016, 64). *Them!* ends with its most contemplative line of thought in the whole film, as Dr. Medford surmises that "when man entered the atomic age, he opened a door into a new world. What we eventually find in that new world, nobody can predict." These coda contextualization statements were common in 1950s science fiction films, and seem to represent their largest attempt at philosophical complexity, but in terms of existential exploration literally come across as too little, too late. Theatergoers would be excused if their lasting impressions of *Them!* was the schlocky action throughout the rest of the film, and not the last second attempt at philosophical musing.

On the alien invasion front, *Earth vs. the Flying Saucers* (1956) represents a common setup and delivery of this era of science fiction media. The opening sequence is a narration that admits to a flying saucer public fervor and "persistent reports of UFOs," and though the film claims that "97% of the objects prove on investigation to be of natural origin" it makes sure to note that "3% still are listed as unknown." Acknowledging that there is "nothing conclusive in the evidence," there is a "widely held belief" that they could be alien, and so the military order is to "fire on sight at any flying objects not identifiable." The narration opines whether this shoot first mentality would be "effective in any battle of *Earth vs. The Flying Saucers*" as the title card appears, which sets up a perfunctory antagonistic film. *Earth vs. the Flying Saucers* is devoid of complex scientific inquiry beyond some brief words by scientist Dr. Russell Marvin about "multiple stage rockets" that can help realize the "ancient dream" of the "exploration of outer space" by humans. The film builds from its antagonism, as the aliens arrive in flying saucers and keep telling Dr. Marvin that they just want to talk or meet, but retaliate to any perceived and real violence against them. Their intentions are not pure, as they announce their plan to invade our planet and absorb our knowledge in order to subjugate humans. Their threat is met with a plan to destroy the aliens and their saucers with a sonic weapon built by Dr. Marvin, because as Vice Admiral Enright says, "When an armed and threatening power lands uninvited in our capital, we don't meet them with tea and cookies." A battle ensues in Washington, DC, and the aliens are defeated using Dr. Marvin's weapon, and the coda contextualization scene on a beach has his wife asking if they will come back again. They both agree that it would not happen again to "such a nice world" that is still here and "still ours," adding to the trend of superficial last second philosophical sentiments unlikely to make a lasting impression on the audience.

Them! and *Earth vs. the Flying Saucers* deal with unintended consequences and external forces, respectively, but there are also many films of this era that engage the "archetypal science fiction impulse of the overreacher, the Faustian figure who effectively barters his soul for knowledge" (Telotte 2001, 89). Noel Carroll describes "four basic movements" of the "Overreacher Plot," from the "preparation for the experiment" to the "experiment itself" to the experiment going "awry, leading to the destruction of innocent victims," and, finally, to "a confrontation with the monster" (1981, 23). Perhaps, the quintessential overreacher 1950s science fiction film is *The Fly* (1958) (Telotte 2001, 193; Weinstock 2014, 49), which combines all of these elements into a potential commentary on the relationship between humans and scientific discovery. The film opens with a lengthy framing device of the overreaching scientist, André Delambre, already dead, apparently killed by his wife, Hélène. After twenty-seven minutes, *The Fly* finally cuts on a shimmer to a few months before André's death and him showing Hélène his new research on matter transportation and his disintegrator-integrator invention. After a series of five "preparation for the experiment" scenes, where André hones his technique from inanimate objects to living things to fulfill this portion of the overreacher plot, Hélène decries that "it's like playing God" and worries about the "suddenness of our age, electronics, rockets, Earth satellites, supersonic flight, and now this." André, caught up in his overreaching, tells her to just accept these things as "part of our normal life." This scene dissolves to a few weeks later, where he continues this thematic complexity, telling Hélène that she is "frightened by progress, I'm filled with the wonder of it." André decides to transport himself, but accidentally splices his DNA with that of a housefly during "the experiment," which has clearly gone "awry." There is budgetary skimping, with the first look at André's fly arm not occurring until fifty-five minutes into the film and the full head reveal not occurring until the seventy-minute mark. André, becoming more clouded in his humanity, tells Hélène that "there are things man should never experiment with," and has her kill him with a hydraulic press to destroy the evidence. Coming back into the present framing device, they find the fly to prove Hélène's innocence, and François delivers the coda contextualization, saying, "He was searching for the truth. He almost found a great truth, but for one instant he was careless," and that the "search for the truth is the most important work in the whole world and the most dangerous." However complex and laudable, there is still a difference between the scientific philosophy musings of *The Fly* and explicitly existential science fiction, as the overreacher plot is often about keeping man in his place not exploring what that place is.

Contained within 1950s science fiction media, Bradley Schauer notes a rise in the form of science fiction subgenre that hid complexity within action-driven plotlines called "political allegory—a form particularly suited to SF, which could safely couch political commentary in the guise of escapist futuristic fantasy" (2016, 59). Although sometimes effective with some filmmakers using "SF allegory as a productive way to deal with contemporary issues without attracting unwanted scrutiny," Schauer caveats that in "many instances, however, the political message is not clear-cut" (2016, 59). The most famous opaque and ambiguous science fiction political allegory is

Invasion of the Body Snatchers (1956), because of its potentially contradictory symbolic messaging. *Body Snatchers* is about a small California town being overrun by alien pods that "have the power to reproduce themselves in the exact likeness of any form of life," including replicating human bodies and minds exactly, but without individualism and emotions. When the two main characters, Dr. Miles Bennell and Becky Driscoll, push back on this notion of an "untroubled world" where "everyone's the same" the broad strokes of the political allegory start to come into relief, but there is conflicting nuance that arises when a narrative does not come right out and state its thematic intention. Reviewer David Wood of the BBC notes the polysemous allegorical potential, saying not only that the "sense of post-war, anti-communist paranoia is acute" but so "is the temptation to view the film as a metaphor for the tyranny of the McCarthy era" despite these two thoughts being contradictory (2001). A similar split in intention versus perception arose with *The Thing from Another World* (1951) that "was typically understood by contemporary critics as an example of anticommunist fervor, with the violent, relentless, amoral Thing as a surrogate for Soviet troops, and the film's last line—'Watch the skies!'—advocating American vigilance against Communist attack," whereas one of the film's screenwriters said it was written to make fun of Cold War paranoia (Schauer 2016, 59). Allegorical content was historically effective at including messages that would not have been acceptable if depicted literally, but this kind of subtlety allows plenty of opportunities for misinterpretations.

CONCLUSION

Nascent philosophical developments within the genre of science fiction media were present during these early decades, but they were rare, fleeting, and uncopied by media that followed in their wake. A successful science fiction film may have contained allusions to existential exploration, such as *Frankenstein*'s discussion of human creation or *Destination Mars*' pioneering spirit, but when studios tried to copy their successes, they leaned into the sensational over the philosophical. *Frankenstein* led to *Frankenstein Meets the Wolf Man* (1943) and eventually to *Abbott and Costello Meet Frankenstein* (1948). Even the political allegorical content would not be enough to steer more heavily into the philosophical, given their opaque messages. If anything can be gleaned from what science fiction "learned" from its early mediated roots, it would be that in some cases there is no substitute for directly engaging with a topic. Schauer notes this shift to the explicit in the subsequent era, saying, "It would not be until the late 1960s that the clandestine politics of allegory would be replaced by more overt sociopolitical content" (2016, 59).

In the next chapter, films like *2001* will be shown to not pull their existential punches, or to couch them within allegories, and though the next era will be shown to have a difficult time jump-starting a trend in this regard, they will lay the groundwork for the contemporary existential science fiction media trend.

Chapter 2

Modern Existential Science Fiction

As established in the previous chapter, other than rare exceptions and some shrouded political allegories, "by the late 1950s, SF was associated almost exclusively with cheap, culturally disreputable horror films" (Schauer 2016, 8). The era that followed is more difficult to speak about in generalities, because this shift to cheaply made content led to "the SF/horror exploitation market shrinking in the early 1960s" and the "SF genre splintered and combined with other existing genres to create new story types" like the comedy parody film (Schauer 2016, 94). This chapter will not explore these subgenres, not because they would be monolithically devoid of existential thought, but because the tendency toward surface-level complexity would be higher. This chapter will also not deeply engage the science fiction shift to television, not because the medium did not present complex genre content, but simply because of constraints in focus with such broad content. In fact, Bradley Schauer argues that "at a time when SF films would never have been considered among the most outstanding examples of their medium, *The Twilight Zone* and *Star Trek* made a strong case for SF's potential as intelligent, adult entertainment" (2016, 98). This chapter will instead look to find the moments when science fiction film broke from its exploitation trend line and embraced the philosophical potentials of its genre. Vivian Sobchack argues that when it is at its best

> the SF film is a film genre which emphasizes actual, extrapolative, or speculative science and the empirical method, interacting in a social context with the lesser emphasized, but still present, transcendentalism of magic and religion, in an attempt to reconcile man with the unknown. (Sobchack 1997, 63)

This chapter will trace the trajectory of the existential science fiction film, picking up at a time when the genre shifted from a near total focus on technological speculation and antagonistic battles with aliens/creatures/enemies to a cinematic space more open to the occasional introspective look at what it means to exist as humans. There are many examples to choose from, but as a way to make the focus of this discussion manageable, I will primarily look at the existential characteristics and thematics in three key films of this time period: *2001: A Space Odyssey* (1968), *Solaris* (1972), and *Blade Runner* (1982). In some ways, these films and others represent a smaller version of the cultural cluster of media texts that have been made over the past ten years or so, albeit in a less concentrated manner. They contain a common refractory quality to their human existential exploration, not quite allegorical but at an abstracted level removed, as they all contain ruminations on the humanity, or lack, of nonhuman entities (*2001*'s HAL, *Solaris*'s visitors, and *Blade Runner*'s replicants). Thomas Morrissey notes the

> tradition of robots exhibiting behaviour that is more humane than that of the humans who made them is common in SF, the most popularly known examples occurring in Isaac Asimov's robot stories and the 'person' of Lt. Commander Data of *Star Trek: the Next Generation*. (2004, 256)

Similarly, Benjamin Schrader discusses Donna Haraway's definition of cyborgs and says that "cyborg hybridity of machine and organism is meant to expose, shift, and destroy the boundaries we have created throughout history meant to separate one another along lines of race, class, gender, and sexuality" and that cyborg imagery "works to disrupt the understanding of ourselves, society, and humanity as a whole" (2019, 821). As a counterexample from the same era(s) in question, the *Alien* film series (1979–present) often contains android and other artificial intelligent entities, but does not leverage those characters to explore questions about their relative humanity, though *Prometheus* (2012) will be discussed as breaking this trend in the final section of this chapter. Similarly, *2001*, *Solaris*, and *Blade Runner*, like the contemporary existential cluster discussion throughout the rest of this book, do not represent a monolithic trend during this era of science fiction, only a genre option that audiences and studios were more hospitable to than in previous eras. After looking at these three films, attention will turn to science fiction near the turn of the century and to the ways in which some films stand as potential precursors to the current existential science fiction media trend.

2001: A SPACE ODYSSEY **(1968)**

The opening chyron of *2001: A Space Odyssey*, "The Dawn of Man," followed by the opening sequences of a group of prehistoric hominids learning to use bones as weapons, influenced by the mysterious appearance of a monolith, sets the stage for a film that is overtly concerned with the existence of humans from an evolutionary perspective.[1] Carrol L. Fry addresses this existential thematic core, saying that the "true meaning of the word 'Odyssey' in the title" is "an evolutionary journey from beast, to technology, to a stage of evolution transcending the physical realm," and that the "image patterns and visual metaphors ...also underscore a central theme of the film: the limits of technology and the nature of humanity" (2003, 333). For instance, the connection between the bone as weapon and human evolution is made visually overt, demonstrated in the much-discussed "elliptical cut from a bone to a spaceship, which connects the shots graphically as well as metaphorically and thematically" (Falsetto 2001, 50). This connection continues in the next sequence, which takes place aboard a commercial space flight indicating that humans in *2001* have evolved past the hominids of the first sequence as well as our present-day space travel capabilities. As a flight attendant moves along the commercial space cabin, a cut to a profile close-up of her walking shows her fighting against the gravitational environment while simultaneously appearing as if she is just learning to walk, visually connecting the theme of evolution once again. The sequences that follow track Dr. Heywood Floyd, chairman of the United States National Council of Astronautics, as he travels from Earth to a lunar outpost that resembles a futuristic airport lounge and then on to Clavius Base to discuss the needed secrecy surrounding a monolith that has appeared on the moon. The ease at which Floyd travels through space and navigates these other spaces echoes the evolved technological mastery of these human beings, and also stands as a contrarian to the often difficult and action-packed space travel depicted in most science fiction media. Floyd and some other astronauts are tasked with examining the lunar monolith, and when they do it emits a high-pitched frequency that hurts their ears, followed by a low-angle shot of the sun peeking over the monolith, visually matching a similar shot from the opening Dawn of Man sequence.

2001 then cuts to eighteen months later and matches the visual shape of the prehistoric bone and the spaceship from Floyd's mission with the "Discovery One" spaceship on the "Jupiter Mission." The themes of human evolution are further highlighted as the sequence opens with Discovery One mission commander, Dr. David Bowman (Dave), jogging on a circular rotating track that produces artificial gravity. This type of spaceship design is quite common in science fiction media, seen in everything from *Babylon 5* (1994–1998) to *Interstellar* (2014) to the video game *Halo: Combat Evolved* (2001), partially because it shows an advanced mastery of space travel but also because it allows for film and television productions to not have to simulate zero gravity for their casts all the time. In this film, *2001*, its use directly at the beginning of the Jupiter Mission sequence connects it directly to the first shots of the stumbling flight attendant during the lunar Floyd sequence, with the jogging Bowman representing a visual "step" forward in human evolution and space travel.

In a BBC broadcast that the crew of the Discovery One are watching, the subject turns to the onboard artificially intelligent computer, HAL 9000 (standing for Heuristically Programmed Algorithmic Computer), which is described as the "latest result in machine intelligence" that can "mimic most of the activities of the human brain, and with incalculably greater speed and reliability." In a nod to the central theme of the film, that of evolutionary progress and intelligence, the BBC broadcast cuts to a taped interview with the HAL 9000, lending credence to its treatment as a sentient, almost human, member of the crew. After the interviewer mentions that the HAL 9000 prefers to just be called "HAL" and saying that it is "brain and central nervous system of the ship," the questions become very human in their tone of inquiry, asking whether HAL ever gets nervous about the responsibility it has for the mission or frustrated by having to rely on a fallible human crew. HAL reassures the interviewer that it does not make mistakes, so that is why it would not be nervous, and that it has a good "relationship" with the crew, both answers validating the emotional inquiries of the interviewer. When the broadcast cuts to an interview with Poole about HAL, he comes right out and says that HAL "really just is another person" on board the ship. When the interviewer presses Poole and asks whether he believes HAL has "genuine emotions," Poole responds that "he acts like he has genuine emotions, um, of course he's programmed that way to make it easier to talk to him." This interplay between machine intelligence, genuine emotions, and an evolved form of humanity will become the primary theme throughout the rest of *2001*. In terms of raw intelligence, there is no human competition with HAL, dramatized quickly in a chess match between Poole and HAL that the computer describes as "enjoyable" but in which the human is clearly outmatched. However, the critique of sentient intelligences is more nuanced, as the subject of evolved emotional depth becomes key to the way *2001* unfolds.

2001 is a film with very little dialogue in comparison to its runtime, with only 40 of the 160 minutes in the film containing dialogue (Fry 2003, 333), signaling a thematic exploration of the relationship between our development of language and our evolution as a species. Fry notes that "the film repeatedly invites us to see the contrast between the sophistication of technology in 2001 and the banality of human conversation" (2003, 337). Much of the antagonism between HAL and Bowman manifests through a very human mechanism, miscommunication and the lack of communication. When Poole and Bowman first suspect that HAL may be malfunctioning, they go into a pod where they think that HAL cannot hear them, though it turns out it was reading their lips through the pod window. Now knowing their intent to shut off its higher brain functions, HAL proceeds to kill Poole while he is out in a pod, and then refuses to talk to Bowman to let him back into Discovery One. Then, once Bowman successfully gets back in via an emergency hatch, he refuses to speak to HAL when he attempts to disconnect it. HAL becomes its most human in this moment, both as a result of Bowman's "silent treatment" and because it repeatedly says, "I'm afraid," at the prospect of being turned off. HAL appears to feel genuine existential dread as it can sense its "mind going, there is no question about it." The repeated phrase from HAL, "I can feel it," seems to be a plea to Bowman that this artificially intelligent computer is a conscious sentient being worthy of pity. After shutting down HAL, Bowman receives a prerecorded message that could only be played for the crew once they reached Jupiter, revealing the true nature of their mission to explore the signal that the lunar monolith sent to Jupiter and furthering the idea of shrouded communications as a source of human strife.

The final section of *2001* begins, entitled "Jupiter and Beyond the Infinite," and along with it the most overtly existential, and trippy, content of the film. Bowman attempts to explore a larger monolith near Jupiter in a pod, but is pulled into what can be described as a combination laser-light show and cosmic tunnel. Describing this sequence, Carrol L. Fry says, "Kubrick draws images from eastern mysticism in portraying transcendence through rebirth to an evolutionary stage beyond technology" (2003, 332–333). Bowman ends up in an ornate bedroom depicted at various stages of his life until he reaches for a monolith at the foot of a bed and becomes the Star Child, a glowing planetary-sized in utero fetus next to the Earth, thus completing the film's human evolution commentary.

Bradley Schauer describes the impact *2001* had on the genre and the film industry as a whole, saying that the

> mountain of critical discourse on Kubrick's film, exploring its philosophical implications, symbolism, and aesthetic merit, led to a broader critical reassessment of SF film. A new generation of critics who grew up watching '50s SF films began to explore their subtextual meanings, making a case for them as intriguing cultural artifacts. (2016, 95)

The important takeaway from *2001* for this book is just how different this version of science fiction is to its previous decade(s), as its "thought-provoking themes about the evolution of mankind and our relationship to technology also made clear to viewers, critics, and film-makers alike that SF cinema could be more than space opera and exploitation horror" (Schauer 2016, 122). The influences of this film were widespread, but there were more changes to come as in "the wake of *2001* and *Planet of the Apes*, SF enjoyed enhanced critical and cultural cachet, but was still not considered a reliable big-budget genre" (Schauer 2016, 9).

SOLARIS (1972) AND *SOLARIS* (2002)

Coming on the heels of *2001*, *Solaris* is a further examination of what it means to be human, this time through the exploration and colonization of a fictional interstellar planet of the same name. This Russian film by Andrei Tarkovsky is adapted from the Stanisław Lem book, also entitled *Solaris* (1961), and works through concepts of existence, memory, intelligent life, and love through astronauts' encounters with the sentient ocean of the planet Solaris. Lem himself says he was trying to "create a vision of a human encounter with something that certainly exists, in a mighty manner perhaps, but cannot be reduced to human concepts, ideas or images" (2002). The book and film adaptations of *Solaris* concern a fictional planet of the same name that is covered by an ocean that appears to be sentient, or at least able to influence the thoughts and experiences of other sentient beings. Lem addresses this mystery, saying that

> one should not speak of a "thinking" or a "non-thinking" Ocean, however the Ocean certainly was active, undertook some voluntary actions and was capable of doing things which were entirely alien to the human domain . . . and entered, in its own way, into minds of the people of the "Solaris" Station and revealed what was deeply hidden in each of them. (2002)

The way these deeply hidden things manifest is through the appearance of people from the crew members' pasts, primarily Kris Kelvin who was sent to the Solaris station decades after it lost contact with Earth. Aboard the station, Kris sees a message from Dr. Gibarian, a crew member who killed himself before Kris's arrival, telling him to "understand that this is not madness. It has something to do with conscience." After Kris encounters Hari, his wife who had died ten years ago, Dr. Snaut tells him that the phenomenon manifests differently for everyone and that what he "saw was the materialization of your conception of her." Snaut says Solaris' ocean probes their minds and creates "islands of memory."

The Hari that Kris encounters on the Solaris station does not remember much, and Kris recognizes her artificiality and jettisons her into space. Vladimir Tumanov says that this first iteration of Hari demonstrates "Locke's philosophy of mind where personhood is identical with memory: this Hari-like being cannot be a human person and must be dispensed with as if it were a disruptive object" (2016, 360). This initial version of Hari is not the last, as she reappears to Kris in a much more fully realized version of how he remembers her. Standing next to Kris and looking at herself in a mirror in an over the shoulder two shot, two versions of both Hari and Kris appear in the frame. She tells Kris that when she closes her eyes she cannot remember her own face, the film's second reference to object permanence and positioning Hari as some kind of developing child. When she asks Kris "Do you know yourself?" he responds that he does, "Like all humans." The composition of this shot is further deepened by droplets of water on the part of the glass that is reflecting Hari, but not on the part reflecting Kris, solidifying the refractory nature of Hari's memory/identity compared to Kris's, as her origin is the combination of the Solaris ocean's and Kris's reconstituted memories.

The question of whether Hari is human/sentient or not becomes the existential nexus of the film, as *Solaris* presents a meditation on consciousness and memory. During a scene that evolves into a discussion about the copy of Hari's humanity, or lack thereof, Snaut says that humans "have no interest in conquering any cosmos" but instead "want to extend the Earth to the borders of the cosmos," and that we do not need other worlds, "we need a mirror." He is echoing a sentiment common in existential science fiction that deals with the reasons that humans would want to explore the cosmos, such as in *Ad Astra* (2019) when a moon base is described as just a "recreation of what we're running from on Earth." Here, the encounter with space and aliens is not politically allegorized as an encounter with Earthly combative forces, such as with the replicants in *Invasion of the Body Snatchers* (1956), but is instead overtly about the internal encounters with one's own memories, life, and humanity. Hari goes on to argue that she is "becoming a human being" not because of origin, but because she "can feel just as deeply as you." She goes on to drop the equivocation, professing, "I am a human being." Snaut dismisses this equivalency of emotions to humanity, echoing some of the sentiments Lem has about both *Solaris* adaptations, saying, "Don't turn a scientific problem into a common love story." In its penultimate sequence, *Solaris* ends its philosophical musings with a discussion between Snaut and Kris that is one of the more explicitly existential scenes in this era of science fiction. Kris begins to ask questions about "the meaning of life," and Snaut contrasts happiness with these kinds of "dire questions," saying that when someone is happy "the meaning of life and other eternal themes rarely interest" them and that these kinds of questions should be saved for "the end of one's life." Kris describes asking questions as "a desire to know," but admits that "the preservation of simple human truths require mystery." The scene ends as the camera gets closer and closer to Kris's ear, as an abstraction of sorts the closer the image grows, and with the sentiment akin to ignorance being bliss when it comes to the end of our lives, as Kris claims that "not knowing" the answers "makes us practically immortal." In the film's coda, Kris is shown to be on one of Solaris' islands of memory, happy to live out his life among his artificial, but there, memories.

Much has been written about what *Solaris* is attempting to say and its lasting impact on the science fiction genre and film in general. One theorist, Steven Dillon, connects the film's medium self-referential nature to its existential nature, pointing to this genre influence. Dillon argues that "Tarkovsky's film has a particular relevance to American film of the 1990s, where amidst a cultural landscape of virtual reality, fantasy takes on an unprecedented significance" (2006, 2). Dillon presents *Solaris* as self-reflexive, saying that it "provides a detailed and complex model for cinematic illusion" and though it "is not explicitly about cinematic illusionism . . . it is a film implicitly about film" (2006, 8). Dillon then brings the philosophical into this argument, discussing cinematic absence and presence and saying that "instead of psychoanalytic identification, *Solaris* emphasizes existential solitude" (2006, 12). Dillon then makes the link between the existential questions posed by the film and this medium self-referentiality, saying that "Hari's identity does not just waver between human and inhuman, between reality and hallucination, but between art and technology" (2006, 13). In the end, *Solaris* is an existential island of sorts, that was influential, just maybe not right away.

Fudging the proposed eras a little bit, I think it is important to discuss the 2002 *Solaris* remake, for the ways in which it is influenced by the original, the novel, as well as by its own unique historical and industrial circumstances. It was made in a turn-of-the-century Hollywood environment that included science fiction films *Star Wars: Episode II: Attack of the Clones*, *Men in Black II*, *Signs*, and *Minority Report* all released and in the top ten at the box office in the same year (Box Office Mojo, n.d.d). Science fiction was very profitable and popular in 2002. So a science fiction film based on a cerebral 1961 Polish novel and a philosophical 1972 Russian film starring one of Hollywood's biggest stars George Clooney does not seem like a natural combination. Given the heuristics of existential exploration and antagonistic/action focus employed throughout this book, the obvious question arises of how *Solaris* (2002) compares to *Solaris* (1972) in these two regards. Though the 2002 remake begins its time in the space station with bloodstains on the floor and tales of security forces shooting up pods, it is roughly equal in its lack of violence and antagonism to the original. Both contain relatively benign unexplained replicating forces from Solaris, and in both versions the entities sacrifice their existences to save the main protagonist Kris/Chris.

In many ways, the 2002 remake builds from the existential explorations of the original film, even going as far as to use the "we don't want other worlds, only mirrors" line near the beginning of the film, almost as a jumping-off point compared to its use at the end of the 1972 version. This line is said just as Chris falls asleep for the first time, which is the triggering device for Solaris to replicate human memories/consciousness. The film then cuts to our first shots of the titular planet, and cuts back to Chris just as the memory mirroring process begins for him with flashback dreams and the replication of his deceased wife, Rheya, standing next to him in bed. Solaris takes what you desire most and materializes it, and for Chris that is the resurrection of his wife, just like in the original film. There are thematic embellishments and concentrations in the remake, as audiences are given a subjective POV look inside the replicated Rheya's mind as she experiences the real Rheya's memories. Speaking about these flashbacks, Dillon argues that Soderbergh "expands on Tarkovsky by visualizing concretely the remembered past" (2006, 42), but the added element of the replicated Rheya's subjective perspective furthers the theme that she is a conscious entity worthy of consideration as human. Rheya later describes her relationship to humanity, avoiding the certainty of Hari's statement that she is definitively a "human being," by saying to Chris that she "came from your memory of her, that's the problem. I'm not a whole person." Miriam Jordan and Julian Jason Haladyn engage with this "disembodied distance between the guest Rheya and the human being Rheya" saying that she begins "constructing a history within the space and time they are located, systematically forming their own reality," granting her a "unique existence" (2010, 268). Dillon describes this overt acknowledgment of the Solaris memory replication process as "Soderbergh's most substantial annotations of Tarkovsky" noting that when Chris says, "I was haunted by the idea that I remembered her wrong," that this "addition is very much in line with the spirit of Tarkovsky's earlier version" (2006, 10). These embellishments, additions, and enhancements of existential themes in the *Solaris* remake represent a potential trend line upward and moment when it might have been possible to begin another cultural cluster of existential science fiction, but an argument could be made when looking at the box office ranking of 2002 that perhaps audiences and the film industry were not ready to spark a new existential cluster. A contemporary review by Stephen Holden explicitly makes this connection, saying that *Solaris* is a "science-fiction film lacking action-adventure sequences" and that its "insistence on remaining cerebral and somber to the end may be a sign of integrity, but it should cost it dearly at the box office" (2002).

BLADE RUNNER (1982) AND *BLADE RUNNER 2049* (2017)

Based on the Philip K. Dick novel, *Do Androids Dream of Electric Sheep?*, and directed by Ridley Scott, *Blade Runner* (1982) exists as potentially one of the most existential science fiction films made during the twentieth century, and is certainly as influential on future science fiction media. The film is made during an interesting era for the science fiction genre, as it is released a few years after "1977's *Star Wars* and *Close Encounters of the Third Kind*, that established SF as the quintessential contemporary blockbuster genre" both having "used high production values, cutting-edge special effects, and a keen sense of verisimilitude and narrative world-building" (Schauer 2016, 9). *Blade Runner* builds from these production characteristics, leveraging them to great effect in terms of its complexity of philosophical thought. The opening chyron reads,

> Early in the 21st Century, THE TYRELL CORPORATION advanced robot evolution into the NEXUS phase—a being virtually identical to a human—known as a Replicant. The NEXUS 6 Replicants were superior in strength and agility, and at least equal in intelligence, to the genetic engineers who created them.

In fact, the Tyrell Corporation's motto goes beyond human equivalency, calling the replicants "More human than humans." The film revolves around a futuristic dystopian Earth, 2019 Los Angeles, where replicants are hunted down by blade runners, primarily Rick Deckard, whose job it is to "retire" them because of their unauthorized existence on Earth (they are used as slave labor "off-world"). Looking, sounding, and acting like human beings, the question for these blade runners is how to determine who is human and who is android. Jori De Coster gets to the heart of why this type of science fiction setup is so effective at presenting philosophical complexity, saying that "human hybrids who stand at the border by incorporating technology raise contemporary questions on their but also our humanity" (2011, 220). These questions only arise because of the inability to quickly and definitively determine who falls into each existential camp.

When in doubt, a test is administered by blade runners, called the Voight-Kampff test, that measures the subjects' responses to a series of hypothetical questions designed to elicit emotional responses, such as "Your little boy shows you his butterfly collection, plus the killing jar. What do you say?" The test is depicted as focusing on an extreme close-up of the subject's eye, and with Dr. Eldon Tyrell asking Deckard whether it measures the "Capillary dilation of the so-called blush response? Fluctuation of the pupil? Involuntary dilation of the iris?" it is clearly more complicated than the often referenced in science fiction "Turing test." Proposed by A. M. Turing, this test is initially described as an "imitation game" whereby "modifying this computer to have an adequate storage, suitably increasing its speed of action, and providing it with an appropriate program" that it could "play satisfactorily" the part of a human without being detected (1997, 38). Described more plainly by John Haugeland, the Turing test is based on the idea that a "system is surely intelligent . . . if it can carry on an ordinary conversation like an ordinary person" (Haugeland 1997, 4). Turing viewed this as a minimum for artificial intelligence, so despite its potential for being "too lenient" it is "elegant" and "compelling" (Haugeland 1997, 3–4). However, for *Blade Runner*, the Voight-Kampff test is designed to be more certain, and the film opens with the administration of the test to a suspected replicant named Leon. Questions begin to fluster Leon, and instead of getting a view of the nuances of the test, he shoots the tester administering the test, confirming he is a replicant. *Blade Runner* quickly makes clear the antagonism that will become an integral part of the android-human science fiction story, with De Coster arguing that "cyborg villains epitomize boundaries of humanness and reflect a specific existential fear that relates to the apocalyptic and dehumanizing aspects of technology" (2011, 220). Deckard, and the other blade runners, are our attempts at human control over an evolved form of our recognizable selves, with De Coster going on to posit that we only "attribute 'evilness' to technology when we tend to loose [sic] control over it or when technology starts to control us and/or when it erodes our humanity" (2011, 221). Beyond Turing or Voight-Kampff in terms of certainty, the question of whether an artificially intelligent being could be considered human arises. It is not just whether the machine can trick humans, but are they cognitively human themselves, as *Blade Runner* is as much about the sentience and existential crises of its inhuman characters, as it is about the human ones. John R. Searle calls this strong AI, arguing that "the appropriately programmed computer really is a mind, in the sense that computers given the right programs can be literally said to *understand* and have other cognitive states" (1980, 417; emphasis in original). A replicant named Pris invokes the Cartesian tenet in this regard, plainly saying, "I think therefore I am."

Theorists have discussed this idea of the replicants as worthy of humanity from a variety of philosophical perspectives. David Desser invokes a humanistic approach, saying that the approach "taken at its most literal, is a way of life centered in human interests which asserts that self-realization is attained through reason, a significant philosophy in this film about human facsimiles, about what it means to be human" (1997, 61–62). Desser describes how "redemption comes to Deckard and Rachel from the humanistic idea of transcendence through love amidst one's own existential condition" (1997, 61). About Roy Batty, Marilyn Gwaltney invokes existential philosophy by arguing that

> our understanding of his cruelty changes as we come to understand it as a very human reaction to his existential situation: the imminence of his death and that

of those he loves; the feeling of betrayal by the beings that brought him into existence. (1997, 33)

Zeb Kaylique, also uses an existential approach, but contrasts humans and replicants in the opposite direction, saying the

> replicants that we encounter in the first Blade Runner film are self-aware and seek age-old answers to the problems of identity and purpose despite the fact that they are born of technology, artificial. They question themselves and seek truth and reassurance. The humans on the other hand, have little time for reflection and emotion. (2019, 218)

Kaylique posits that the existential message of the *Blade Runner* films is that it "does not matter where we come from or who we are, all that matters are the decisions we make and the way we choose to live our lives," and that the "people we meet, the things we care about, and the causes we deem worthy, ultimately define our personal construction of meaning" (2019, 222). Discussing the novel source material, Robert Scholes and Eric Rabkin layer in another level of existence, saying, "If androids dream of electric sheep, then aren't they really human? And if they're human, and if we've created them, then are we gods? Or meddling fools?" (1977, 180).

It is worthwhile to discuss and compare the sequel film, *Blade Runner 2049* (2017), despite the fact that it belongs in subsequent chapters by strict chronology, for the ways in which it extends, enhances, or detracts from the existential explorations of the original film. The opening chyron of *2049* immediately makes the question of replicant humanity less equivocal, given that the original used the language "virtually identical to a human" and the sequel simply calls the replicants "bioengineered humans." There are many new elements, replacing the Voight-Kampf with the "baseline test" and adding in virtual projected AI entities, but much of the existential critique of what constitutes humanity remains. The primary protagonist, KD6-3.7 or K, is unequivocally replicant, and is searching for meaning and love in his life. The primary AI entity, and love interest for K, is the holographic Joi, who appears to have her own longings to be human and corporeal. When K gets an "emanator" that allows him to take Joi outside for the first time, suddenly, the always raining environment of *Blade Runner*'s Los Angeles becomes an asset, given that Joi is able to feel an all-encompassing sensory touch experience. Speaking to the existential ruminations in *2049*, Silke Arnold-de Simine describes how characters like Joi's various engagements with memory and identity help to "recognize and explore memory play as an alternative mode of recall and remembrance as well as a potentially vital part of 'memory activism'" (2019, 71). Memories were manipulable in the original film, but the process itself is shown in *2049*. K visits a replicant memory designer, Dr. Ana Stelline, as she dials in and creates the expressions of children at a birthday party out of thin air. She tells K that "if you have authentic memories, you have real human responses" and that "we recall with our feelings, anything real should be a mess." Memories become assets that can either prove or disprove your humanity or status.

Blade Runner 2049 is also about the search for meaning and purpose, a very existentialism friendly theme, as the replicants look to rally around something, with replicant freedom fighter Freysa telling K, "Dying for the right cause, it's the most human thing we can do." Sean Guynes links this goal to the existential theme of the film, arguing that "the replicants seek a saviour to prove, in some sense, their humanity" (2020, 146). The rallying mechanism is a replicant, Rachel from the original film, who became pregnant and birthed a child, extending creation to replicants as an important cornerstone to their developing humanity. Freysa tells K, "I knew that baby meant we are more than just slaves. If a baby can come from one of us, we are our own masters." This type of creation is contrasted in *2049* with that of the Wallace Corporation's, Tyrell's successor. We see a replicant born from a plastic bag, and Wallace Corporation CEO, Niander Wallace, remarks that he wants to discover the secret to the replicant reproduction solely to expand colonization efforts. Guynes calls the competing goals of Wallace and the replicants the "heterosexual culmination of capitalist fantasies of an endless supply of (genetically non-human) slave labour, and, at the same time as a revolutionary fantasy of the android underclass's desire to free themselves from human control" (2020, 145). The idea behind replicants rallying around the born replicant child, who turns out to be the memory maker Dr. Ana Stelline, is that it puts the definition and status of existence wholly within the control of the replicants and not their human makers. When K sees a dog with Deckard, he asks, "Is it real?," to which Deckard replies, "I don't know, ask him." For *2049*, being real, human, is up to the person, dog, themselves.

CONTEMPORARY EXISTENTIAL PRECURSORS

It is not that the rest of the science fiction films of the 1980s and 1990s do not contain existential content, just that for the sake of brevity, I am going to lean on Schauer's argument that the "surprise success of *Star Wars* led to a dramatic reconfiguration of the major film studios' approach to SF" with an "unabashed embrace of old SF tropes like robots, space battles, and grotesque aliens" (2016, 2). Tracking main forms of science fiction through these eras, roughly built around ratings designations, Schauer presents a less than existential view of the genre at this time. This next section will look at a few films from the early twenty-first century that begin to shift the philosophical balance and set up the contemporary trend of existential science fiction.

One of the most explicitly existential films made during this era is *A.I.: Artificial Intelligence* (2001), extending the thematic discussion about the humanity of robots and androids brought forth in previous works like *Metropolis*, *2001*, and *Blade Runner*. This film was directed by Steven Spielberg, but was originally developed by Stanley Kubrick and so retains much of the same existential exploration of human evolution into artificial intelligence that HAL represented in *2001*. Structured around the story of Pinocchio, Thomas Morrissey calls it an unsuccessful blend of "Collodi's and Kubrick's hard-boiled realism with Spielberg's sentimentality" in an attempt to engage "a classic dystopian theme—the horror of enforced, perpetual childhood—set adrift" (2004, 250). The film opens on the premise that global warming and rising sea levels created the need for "legal sanctions to strictly licensed pregnancies." So Professor Allen Hobby is shown telling a group of students that the goal to "create an artificial being has been a dream of man since the birth of science," and though the current "artificial being is a reality of perfect simulacrum, articulated in limb, articulate in speech, and not lacking in human response. . . . We are rightly proud of it, but what does it amount to?" To fill an emotional void of the sanctions, Hobby says, "I propose that we build a robot child who can love. A robot child who will genuinely love the parent or parents it imprints on, with a love that will never end." Genuine love would certainly qualify as Searle's definition of "strong AI" if the android could be "literally said to *understand* and have other cognitive states" (1980, 417; emphasis in original). Hobby goes on to describe an android, which he calls "a Mecha with a mind, with neuronal feedback," where "love will be the key by which they acquire a kind of subconscious. Never before achieved. An inner world of metaphor, of intuition, of self-motivated reasoning, of dreams." A foreshadowing student asks Hobby, "If a robot could genuinely love a person, what responsibility does that person hold toward that Mecha in return?"

Obviously, they create such an android child, whom they call David, and as a commercial for him states, "His love is real but he is not," hinting that *A.I.* blunts the film's position on android-human equivalency. A couple who work for the android manufacturing company, Henry and Monica, have a human child in a seemingly irrecoverable coma, so David is given to them as a trial run. Unlike other versions of this same story of humanity within androids, such as in *Blade Runner* or *Ex Machina*, the initial impressions of the artificially intelligent robots in *A.I.* are recognizable as such. David, the child robot, moves mechanically and talks monotonously, that is until Monica performs the imprinting procedure, and love is added to the equation. Suddenly, David becomes much more humanlike in his mannerisms, speech, and movements. He develops a deep love for Monica, his "mommy," but also accompanying emotions like jealousy and hate, which intensify when their human child, Martin, wakes from his coma and comes home. David begins to make mistakes, almost accidentally killing Martin, so the decision is made to take David back to the manufacturer where he will be destroyed. When Monica abandons David in the forest to save him from being destroyed, he says, "I'm sorry I'm not real," and asks if he can come home if he becomes real like Pinocchio. In subsequent sequences, *A.I.* begins to introduce pushback against the idea of androids as the next step in human evolution. There is a "Flesh Fair" sequence where humans destroy Mechas to reassert their dominance. An announcer yells about a "commitment to a truly human future" while robots are shot from cannons through rings of fire. The announcer at the fair sees David and dismisses him as "one of those built to aspire to the human condition."

A.I. transitions into David's ceaseless search for the Blue Fairy to turn him into a real boy, and ends as a commentary on the future of humanity. David makes his way to a flooded New York City, and finds Hobby and another version of himself, which enrages David as he yells, "I'm special, I'm unique." David tells Hobby he hoped the Blue Fairy would "make me a real boy," to which Hobby responds that "you are a real boy, at least as real as I've ever made one."

He says they were testing David to see

> where would your self-motivated reasoning take you, to the logical conclusion. The Blue Fairy is part of the great human flaw to wish for things that don't exist or to the greatest single human gift, the ability to chase down our dreams, and that is something no machine has ever done until you.

David's search for reality and love was a product of beta test, as Hobby tells him he is not "one of a kind" but the "first of a kind." David is not comforted by this and takes a ship to the underwater Coney Island and a statue of the Blue Fairy, but is trapped by a falling Wonder Wheel. "2000 years passed by" and David is pulled from the ice by a group of super-evolved Mechas looking to study humans, who have become extinct. Because David knew living humans, he is called "the enduring memory of the human race" and "the most lasting proof of their genius." In a moonlit shot of a super-evolved Mecha and David, the discussion turns explicitly existential, with the evolved being describing how "human beings created a million explanations of the meaning of life" and they surmised that "certainly, human beings must be the key to the meaning of existence" so they sought to recreate human life itself. However, these evolved beings were only successful in recreating the dead for one single day. Once they fell asleep and lost consciousness that first day, they died again. David gets to spend one day with the revived genetic memory of Monica, and the film ends with the idea that despite the super-evolved androids, there is something irreplaceable about human existence.

Initially coming across as a mumblecore indie romance where a man named Joel and a woman named Clementine dated and then broke up, *Eternal Sunshine of the Spotless Mind* (2004) does not feel anything like a typical science fiction film until Joel is handed a card from a company called Lacuna Inc. that says, "Clementine Kruczynski has had Joel Barish erased from her memory. Please never mention their relationship to her again." Semantically, the science fiction within *Eternal Sunshine* comes solely from a future technological process by which anyone can have someone from their lives completely erased from their memories. Joel decides to also have Clementine erased from his memory, and is told by the head of Lacuna, Dr. Howard Mierzwiak, to gather all the objects in his life associated with her so they can "use these items to create a map of Clementine in your brain" and "after the mapping is done, our technicians will do the erasing in your home tonight." Writer Charlie Kaufman, who also wrote the similarly surreal and memory/identity-focused *Being John Malkovich* (1999), recognizes the generic elements but feels they are subservient to the emotional core of the film, saying that "*Malkovich* and this have supernatural kinds of elements" but "I don't think of it as science fiction" (Cohen 2016).

Certainly not the purest science fiction film from a semantic perspective, but *Eternal Sunshine* leverages this high concept to steer into syntactic existential themes of memory and identity. The film consists of a series of memory vignettes, where Lacuna techs erase Clementine from Joel's memory in reverse chronological order. Because of this narrative structure of a relationship gone wrong shown in reverse, the memories become increasingly happy and Joel begins to regret the memory erasure. *Eternal Sunshine* begins working on the theme of the malleability of memories when our perceptions about a topic or person change, even working in the Nietzsche quote, "Blessed are the forgetful, for they get the better even of their blunders." Joel tries, unsuccessfully, to sabotage and stop the process, but is able to subconsciously hang onto the phrase "Meet me in Mantauk." The film ends with both characters being confronted with the truth of their memory erasure, and made to listen to each other's thoughts prior to the procedure, which are used as a mechanism to comment on the continuity of thought and how memories change over time. *Eternal Sunshine* ends by repeating again and again a shot of Joel and Clementine running on a snowy beach as it fades to white, highlighting the cyclical nature of human behavior.

Prometheus (2012) finds itself at the cusp of an era shift, as defined by this book, as it is posited that *Gravity* released a year later kicks off the current existential science fiction trend. However, *Prometheus* should be given some credit in this regard, as a film that exists within a franchise, *Alien*, that though it contained numerous androids and aliens-spliced with human DNA had never previously delved deep into existential implications of these characters. Made in a different era than its franchise predecessors, *Prometheus* exists in a much more hospitable audience and industrial environment to leverage the science fiction genre to explore these existential questions. The film opens on a humanoid protohuman "seeding" a barren planet with its own DNA in order to jump-start life, followed shortly after by a sequence of an android tasked with monitoring a cryogenically sleeping human crew while keeping busy doing very human things like playing basketball, riding a bike, eating, watching/quoting movies, and styling his hair. The crew wakes up when reaching their destination, and receive a holographic message from the supposedly "long dead" Peter Weyland. As Weyland addresses the crew, he singles out a stoically smiling David whom he refers to as the "closest thing to a son I will ever have," but says that "unfortunately he is not human" and though he is immortal he is "unable to appreciate these remarkable gifts because that would require the one thing that David will never have, a soul." David's expression changes only slightly at this stinging remark, though as audiences we have already seen him appreciating humanity through his actions while the crew was asleep. Weyland goes on to discuss the purpose of the mission, to explore the questions of humanity's origins, purpose, and potential afterlife. Weyland introduces the two doctors in charge of the mission, Shaw and Holloway, to explore a moon that may hold the secrets to who we are and how we came to be in the universe.

Prometheus is about this ultimate question of humanity's origins, but places deference to humanity's nesting creation of artificial intelligence in David. This is not a surprise, given that Ridley Scott directed *Prometheus* as well as *Blade Runner* and *Alien*, all of which contain varying levels of android-humanity exploration. As *Prometheus* progresses, the crew does find evidence that the protohumans, whom they refer to as the "engineers," seeded life on Earth. They find the head of an engineer, and objectively determine that they are human at a molecular level, given that their DNA is analyzed and determined to be a match to human DNA. This is already a literal existential moment in the film, but layered on top of this discovery is that David is the one shown to most understand these revelations and to drive the plot forward in key ways. When Holloway talks to David about why the engineers made humans, David counters by asking why humans made him. Holloway replies, "We made you cause we could," to which David replies, "Can you imagine how disappointing it would be for you, to hear the same thing from your creator?" David then proceeds to plant a drop of the engineer seeding material in Holloway's glass, the implication being that he does so out of his disdain for his own creators. If *Prometheus* is about overreaching scientists trying to answer the most profound questions about the origins of humanity and our place in the universe, it is significant that the most cinematic depiction of those answers is shown to David while no other humans are present. David is surrounded by visualizations of planets and the plan of the engineers is laid bare for him alone, ending with him holding a visualization of Earth in his hands. For a different reason, that being the sole living engineer attacking everyone when he is awoken, David is later shown to be the only sentient being around to see the engineer actually use their ship's technology. There are limits to this deference, however, as *Prometheus* reestablishes humanity's dominance in the end. The engineers were planning on returning to destroy humanity, by bringing a version of the *Alien* xenomorphs to Earth, but were stopped by the crew and Shaw, the sole human survivor along with David. Shaw tells David she wants to go to the engineers' home planet instead of home to Earth, because "they created us, then they tried to kill us. They changed their minds, I deserve to know why." David says, "I don't understand," to which Shaw responds, "Well, I guess that's because I'm a human being and you're a robot," reasserting human supremacy in the face of increasing android equivalency.

The next chapter will place *Gravity* at the forefront of this existential science fiction trend, but as mentioned *Prometheus* seems positioned to be influential as well, given that within its own franchise it introduced a healthy amount of existential exploration. Its influence seems evident when looking briefly at its direct successor, *Alien: Covenant* (2017). The film opens on David's eye, and a flashback scene about him being created by Weyland who says, "The only question that matters" is "where do we come from?" David later tells another android named Walter about Weyland, saying, "He was human, entirely unworthy of his creation," but Walter counters back to David that "you were too human, too idiosyncratic, thinking for yourself. Made people uncomfortable." In the end, though, there are limits to existential thought within any trend, film, or franchise, especially given its *Alien* roots, as *Covenant* leverages all of this existential complexity with David more in service of a heel turn villain reveal, much like the original film in the franchise. This, perhaps, will hint at the ways in which the current trend of existential science fiction media may have its own limit or cyclical end date.

CONCLUSION

At the end of *Prometheus*, Weyland says, "We're so close to answering the most meaningful questions ever asked by mankind." The incredibly varied and shifting eras discussed in this chapter, in some ways, model this statement. *2001*, *Solaris*, *Blade Runner*, and some notable more recent films like *A.I.* and *Eternal Sunshine* sought to explore some of these meaningful existential questions, but were seemingly unable to spark the beginnings of a trend like this book is arguing to have been occurring over the past ten years. Perhaps with an entry into a franchise that was never particularly existential, *Prometheus*, coupled with other more philosophically minded science fiction media, the shift away from "old SF tropes like robots, space battles, and grotesque aliens" could occur (Schauer 2016, 2).

NOTE

1. In the concurrent novel written by Arthur C. Clarke, this is described as the "tools they have been programmed to use" by the monoliths (2016, 18).

Chapter 3

Gravity, Ad Astra, and Generational Connections

Whether the contemporary trend of existential science fiction started in earnest with *Gravity* (2013), or *Prometheus* (2012) opened the door for this kind of content, or some other media text was more influential is not entirely important. These texts represent audiences, players, and media industries being more receptive to science fiction content less concerned with antagonistic action and more concerned with philosophy and humanity. This chapter will explore *Gravity* in detail, not only because it contains the existential characteristics that would become hallmarks of this trend but also because it contains the clear semantics of science fiction and combines those with the syntactic themes of connections across generations—a powerful existential combination. This film's analysis will be paired with an exploration of *Ad Astra* (2019), which is likely not the last film in the current existential science fiction trend, but represents one of the most recent entries. Because of its recency, *Ad Astra* may be able to provide some sense of how the existential science fiction media text has, or has not, evolved over the past decade or so. *Ad Astra* also contains a deep generational existential exploration, which puts it nicely in line with the thematics of *Gravity*. Finally, both films are also primarily, though not exclusively, solo missions in space, which provides some significant moments of connection about the human condition and the formation of our identities.

GRAVITY (2013)

When looking at trend lines and cultural clusters of media texts that connect to similar themes, it is helpful to find the beginning, if only because it is sometimes difficult to find the end. For existential science fiction media, where the focus is more on the struggle of existence instead of a struggle against an evil antagonist, the film *Gravity* (2013) stands out as a potential starting point for this particular cluster. This is not to say that once *Gravity* became a success, that suddenly all of Hollywood only wanted to create cerebral science fiction films, replacing villains with philosophical underpinnings. However, it is important to note that the film not only was a critical success, being nominated for ten Academy Awards, but was also a significant box office draw as the eighth highest worldwide grossing film of 2013 (Box Office Mojo, n.d.a). Within the top ten grossing films that year, *Gravity* was also the only film that is not part of a film franchise, which might potentially speak to its originality and existential science fiction influence. The year after *Gravity*'s successes, *Interstellar* (2014) is released to similar critical acclaim and financial success, which points to an industrial media environment more hospitable to these types of narratives. There were still plenty of big-budget franchise science fiction and laser-heavy space battles in subsequent years, but a space had been made for a different kind of science fiction media text.

Gravity (2013) revolves around one astronaut's fight to survive the punishing environment of space after she is separated from her space shuttle by some debris from exploded satellites. Dr. Ryan Stone is tasked with repairing and upgrading the Hubble telescope, aided by veteran astronaut Matt Kowalski, when the unexpected debris destroys their Explorer space shuttle and sends the two of them careening into space. Kowalski tows Stone to the International Space Station (ISS) in his Manned Maneuvering Unit, but runs out of nitrogen propellant and floats out into space to die. Stone is left alone to navigate from the ISS to the Chinese Tiangong space station, where she is able to board a reentry capsule and make it safely back to Earth. Using the antagonist heuristic, *Gravity* contains no real villains, evils, or protagonist adversaries, beyond the nature of space itself and the randomness of the "full on chain reaction" of debris caused by the "unintentional side effect of the Russians striking one of their own satellites." Sure, the choice of Russia is likely intentional to create pseudo-implicit audience antagonism, but narratively the only protagonist barriers are things like physics, temperature, and oxygen. One illusory way in which the film accomplishes the task of focusing on scientific fidelity is through "many shots ranging from 10 to 17 minutes in length, and featuring open-ended camera movement across a highly photorealistic and potentially infinite diegetic space," which "emphatically showcases key capabilities of the digital long take" (Purse 2017, 221–222). This leaves a lot of breathing room for existential thematic exploration, even as *Gravity* appears on the surface to be mostly concerned with the pure action of being marooned in space. The director, Alfonso Cuarón, describes the theme of *Gravity* as "adversity" with the goal to "take it to an extreme place where there's nothing" like space (Rose 2014). *Gravity* begins with the chyron,

"At 600km above planet Earth the temperature fluctuates between +258 and -148 degrees Fahrenheit, there is nothing to carry sound, no air pressure, no oxygen, life in space is impossible." The film uses this opening statement as the foundation for a narrative that leverages the simplicity of the punishing nature of space to make a commentary on the random but connected nature of existence. Arturo Morales-Campos describes the contrast inherent in the presentation of rational space and the themes of the film, arguing, "the scientific–technological environment in which the visual text's diegesis repeatedly finds its opposite in a possibility of return to the human essentials: life" (2016, 9). I would also argue that this contrast is sometimes the most crucial element of existential science fiction, as it allows audiences to focus more intently on the philosophical elements without the distracting sensational and implausible action so prevalent in early science fiction media.

With only two real on-screen characters in *Gravity*, one of which ostensibly goes away thirty minutes into the film, the groundwork for existential exploration falls to a few pivotal key moments, all of which are concerned with generational connections. The first of which is when Kowalski is towing Stone to the ISS and she reveals to him, "I had a daughter, she was four. She was at school playing tag, slipped, hit her head, and that was it. Stupidest thing." Stone describes how she found out while driving, so now she does nothing but "wake up, I go to work, and I just drive." She is frozen in stasis in her life on Earth, and frozen in the recesses of space now. However, if just having a deceased loved one and fighting hard to survive were the only criteria for being considered an existential media text, this book might need to be ten times its current length. Layered on top of all of this action and standard loss as character development, there are many existential themes throughout *Gravity*. First, and foremost, is the theme of literal existence, or the persistence of the human spirit and will to live in the face of the randomness of survival in a chaotic world (universe). Stone's daughter died by random accident, much in the opposite way that Stone is surviving this disaster in space due to randomness, including whether or not her body or survival apparatuses get struck by the thousands of pieces of scattered debris that keep orbiting back around every ninety minutes. On its own, this existential theme might raise *Gravity* to the level of *The Martian*, but the film weaves the elements of the loss of Stone's daughter and random survival into a commentary on the ways in which we can either choose to live or just exist.

The second, and most explicitly existential, sequence that contains *Gravity*'s core thematic elements comes when Stone attempts to use the ISS Soyuz escape pod to reach the Chinese Tiangong space station, but finds it without fuel. She tries to reach Houston via AM radio, but is only able to connect to someone on Earth who cannot possibly help her. Stone talks with an "Inuit fisherman stationed on a remote fjord in Greenland," and though there is miscommunication between the two because of a language barrier, a short film entitled *Aningaaq* (2013) was produced as a companion piece to *Gravity* where you can hear and see the other side of the conversation (Abramovitch 2013). She begins to come to grips with her mortality during their conversation, as she howls along with dogs on the other end of the radio, saying, "I know, we're all gonna die everybody knows that, but I'm gonna die today." Stone works through her existential isolation, worrying that no one will "mourn for me, no one will pray for my soul." Hearing a baby's coos over the radio frequency, and the father singing them a lullaby, Stone decides to give up in the hopes of dying and seeing her daughter, so she turns off the oxygen in the ISS Soyuz escape pod so that she will succumb to a peaceful death. In both instances, the appeal to prayers for her soul and in the decision to give up for a chance to see her deceased daughter, Stone is defining her existence externally, which is counter to the philosophy of existentialism proper. Jean-Paul Sartre defines "the first principle of existentialism" as "existence preceding essence" where as beings we exist before we can be defined by existence (2007, 22). Calling it an "Atheistic existentialism," Sartre counterposes a reliance on God to define our existence and a self-defined version, saying, "Just as he wills himself to be after being thrown into existence, man is nothing other than what he makes of himself" (2007, 22). The lack of oxygen causes her to hallucinate Kowalski knocking on the window and coming in the Soyuz with her, as he tells her that despite her unimaginable loss she has to make a decision to "plant both your feet on the ground and start living life." Stone comes out of her oxygen deprived fog, and makes the decision to push forward and live her life. Like Sartre, Thomas Flynn also puts the existential onus on the individual, arguing that "for the existentialist, the value and meaning of each temporal dimension of lived time is a function of our attitudes and choices," which is "made concrete by how we handle our immersion in the everyday" (2006, 5–6). In the hallucination, Kowalski tells her to use the Soyuz's soft landing rockets to propel her to the Chinese Tiangong space station, but given the illusory nature of Kowalski in this scene, it is obviously Stone herself who has come up with this lifesaving idea.

Though technically alive, Stone was living a shadow of her existence and must now make the choice to reclaim her life, through her own agency, and not external forces and memories. Cuarón may have described the central theme of *Gravity* as being "adversity," but he has also described the ways in which the film is about "rebirth" in that way that it can be "metaphorical in the sense of gaining a new knowledge of ourselves" (Woerner 2013). Morales-Campos describes this "renacer" or rebirth in *Gravity*, as Stone having to go "volver al origen" or back to the origin of herself (2016, 21). Stone has to be reborn into a new person who can accept, or at least live with, the death of her daughter. Cuarón describes Stone as "a character that is drifting metaphorical and literally, drifting towards the void. A victim of their own inertia. Getting farther and farther away from Earth where life and human connections are" (Woerner 2013). This drifting is presented visually and symbolically through the environment of space, as well as the relative safety of the various space station capsules, most overtly in the shot that follows her first entry into the ISS. Stone enters the airlock, takes off her space suit, revels in the warmth and oxygen-rich safe environment, and bends into a zero-gravity fetal position while the tether rope that saved her life symbolically floats from behind her navel area (figure 3.1).

Cuarón describes how *Gravity* is about reconnecting with the "amazing side of life, that keeps us alive. Even if inside you feel you want to die, there's a bigger life impulse that keeps us alive" (Woerner 2013). So Stone cannot stay in the womb of space because she will literally freeze to death (or suffocate or get pulverized by satellite debris), and she cannot go on just existing in her life on Earth as well because that is not really living. Instead, she must emerge from all of this seemingly random adversity a new woman, one defined by her own essence and owning the past that has got her to this point. A kind of intergenerational identity is forged out of the ashes of the shell of her former existence.

This syntactic existential theme is further symbolized in the final scene of *Gravity*, which sees Stone plummeting to the Earth in the Shenzhou capsule that she entered from the Chinese Tiangong space station. Stone embraces the randomness of life and tragedy, broadcasting to Houston "in the blind," that whether she lives or dies in this reentry "it will be one hell of a ride. I'm ready." The capsule crashes into a body of water, and though Houston comes over the radio to indicate they are sending a rescue mission, Stone must still save herself again. Not only does the sinking capsule fill with water,

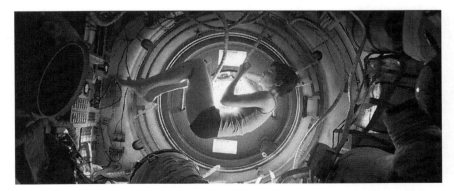

Figure 3.1 The Womb-Like Safety of the International Space Station Represents the Need for Dr. Ryan Stone to Be Reborn in *Gravity* into Someone Capable of Handling Life's Tragedies. *Source*: Gravity (2013). Screenshot taken by author.

furthering a rebirth theme coupled with baptismal symbolism, but Stone must escape her space suit, the lifesaving space skin that must now be shed, to avoid drowning. Stone emerges out of the water a completely different person, made that way by embracing her own internal experiences and tragedies. Stone swims to shore and literally drags her exhausted body into the shoreline sand, and in the final shot of the film she symbolically rises to actualize as this new person. Cuarón makes a direct evolution connection, saying,

> She's in these murky waters almost like an amniotic fluid or a primordial soup. In which you see amphibians swimming. She crawls out of the water, not unlike early creatures in evolution. And then she goes on all fours. And after going on all fours she's a bit curved until she is completely erect. It was the evolution of life in one, quick shot. (Woerner 2013)

Explicitly existential in its thematic content and focused on these explorations of life, humanity, memory, and loss over some form of villainous antagonist, *Gravity* paved the way for more existential science fiction media in the years that followed. Other films like *Interstellar* (2014) and *Arrival* (2016), which will be paired and explored in the next chapter, adopt many of the same thematic characteristics as *Gravity*. Films within a genre that contains inherent exploration potentials that leverage the semantics of science fiction to tell stories about intergenerational connections and loss as a way to examine humanity and existence.

AD ASTRA (2019)

At the most current stage of this existential science fiction trend, *Ad Astra* also contains similar semantic science fiction elements and syntactic generational and philosophical underpinnings, demonstrating the lasting power of this combination. The title is a Latin phrase meaning "to the stars," and the film is about humanity's desire to find extraterrestrial life as a way to define our species in relation to the universe as a whole. Further aligning itself with a scientific fidelity ethos that will be shown in the next chapter to be important to films like *Interstellar*, Director James Gray says, "What I'm trying to do is the most realistic depiction of space travel that's been put in a movie" (Chitwood 2017). This sentiment harkens back to early 1950s science fiction films like *Destination Moon* (1950) that espoused this goal of scientific fidelity, but was abandoned for more exploitative and profitable content. *Ad Astra* uses this scientific fidelity, almost devoid of sensational antagonism beyond a brief lunar rover chase and a rageful baboon, as a rational backdrop to highlight its philosophical content. Amy Karofsky and Mary M. Litch discuss the connection that the main character of *Ad Astra*, Major Roy McBride, has with what Jean-Paul Sartre calls atheistic existentialism, so that the meaning he generates in his life must come from within himself (2021, 240). Roy's conflict, and *Ad Astra*'s to a large degree, has to do with the idea of generational influence, and whether Roy is destined to become like his father. Connecting back to the same Sartre atheistic existentialism tenet of "existence precedes essence" discussed with *Gravity*, *Ad Astra* works through the thematic condition of humanity where in that no prior influence, God or man, predefines someone, but instead that a person "materializes in the world, encounters himself, and only afterwards defines himself" (2007, 22). Calling this the "first principle of existentialism," Sartre goes on to say that a person is "that which he wills himself to be" and "nothing other than what he makes of himself" (2007, 22).

Beginning with a chyron stating, "The near future. A time of both hope and conflict. Humanity looks to the stars for intelligent life and the promise of progress," *Ad Astra* sets up a dichotomy of whether humanity can and should define itself externally, through extraterrestrial contact, or internally, through ourselves. The film begins with a shot of Earth from space, and a cut to Major Roy McBride apparently falling in a space suit, overlaid with the audio of a prescribed mantra that will become a theme throughout *Ad Astra*:

> I am calm, steady. I slept well, 8.2 hours, no bad dreams. I am ready to go, ready to do my job to the best of my abilities. I am focused on only the essential, to the exclusion of all else. I will make only pragmatic decisions. I will not allow myself to be distracted. I will not allow my mind to linger on that which is unimportant. I will not rely on anyone or anything. I will not be vulnerable to mistakes. Resting BPM 47. Submit.

Roy's delivery of these lines is monotone, almost robotic, in nature, and are used as a "psychological evaluation" along with other factors of calmness to prove his worthiness of space exploration. In this opening sequence, they also punctuate a major existential theme within *Ad Astra*, the ways in which we allow or restrict connections to our humanity and whether those connections are valued in society (and in this case, space travel). These lines are crosscut between Roy, head slightly down, speaking in a dark room, and his wife appearing to leave him. In between the word "unimportant" and the statement about not relying on anyone, she is shown blurry, deep in the background, putting what appear to be keys on a counter and walking out of a house. Roy is shown to be the ideal astronaut because he resists outside influences, stressors, and personal connections. He says that he has "always wanted to become an astronaut, for the future of mankind and all, at least that's what I always told myself," but as he walks in a POV shot inside a space suit, greeting others, he adds that "I see myself from the outside. Smile, present a side. It's a performance, with my eye on the exit, always on the exit. Just don't touch me." As Roy finishes this soliloquy about his solitude, he steps out onto a platform of a tower, called the International Space Antenna, built from Earth's surface into the upper atmosphere as he climbs down a ladder with a view of Earth's surface from above. He is alone, not even in a spacecraft, caught between Earth and space, and he describes this experience as "comfortable." Roy is so comfortable, that when the towers begin exploding, sending all the other astronauts climbing the ladders plummeting to their deaths, he is able to avoid blacking out while falling from the stratosphere in a "spin" because of his level of concentration, and then stabilize once closer to the surface so he can deploy his parachute and survive. After this fall, Roy remarks that his wife used to tell him he had a "self-destructive side," and that he "should feel something. I survived, I should feel something." This type of internal monologue sentiment is common in *Ad Astra*, as Roy seems acutely aware of his own internal nature, later saying, "I've been trained to compartmentalize. Seems to me that's how I approach my life."

Roy is brought into a military conference room to discuss his father, H. Clifford McBride, who was the captain of the first manned mission to our outer solar system, the Lima Project, but never returned. The conversation begins with discussions of Roy's calmness, and he is told that the "rumor is that your pulse rate has never gone above eighty, in any of the space walks, sky walks, and even in this most recent fall" and it is remarked that this is "very impressive." The conversation turns to the real purpose of the meeting, as Roy is told about "cosmic ray bursts" from Neptune that have "released high energy particles that caused a catastrophic power surge all over the world" and set to cause a "potentially unstoppable chain reaction" that could "ultimately threaten the stability of our entire solar system." While being questioned and asked how he "handled your father's absence," others in the conference room not so subtly measure and take notes on his reaction, but he calmly states that his "mother was certainly distressed" and that he is sure being away "was very difficult for him as well." Roy is informed that his father is still alive, and may be causing the surges of antimatter causing the catastrophes on Earth. He is told he must travel to Mars, where at a secure outpost he can send a message to his father, and that a "personal plea from you to your father might elicit a response." Here Roy is being recruited both because of his innate ability to resist outside influences and connections, as well as because of his familial connection with his father near Neptune. He is told by a former colleague of his father's, Colonel Thomas Pruitt, that he is "going to be monitored constantly, your mental state, your emotional state. You have a direct connection with the subject." But any attempts to get Roy to admit the connection between the mission and his emotions associated with his father are met with cold pragmatism, especially when confronted with the possibility that his father is responsible for the surges. In fact, the closest Roy comes to showing emotion toward his father is when anyone questions his heroism, saying to try and "impugn a man who has given his entire life" to the space program is "despicable, desperate at best."

The mission is broken up into three parts: first, Roy must travel "commercial" with Pruitt to the moon so as to avoid causing a panic; once there, he then has to make his way to the SpaceCom base where the long range rocket Cepheus can take him to Mars; and once on Mars, he will send a series of messages to his father near Neptune. The travel sequence to the moon resembles any present-day airline terrestrial travel, with an overt commentary on overcommercialization. When Roy asks for a "blanket and pillow" pack onboard the flight to the moon, he is told that it will cost him $125, and is reminded that the moon is "borderless" with many disputed mining war zones. Roy arrives in the Moon terminal, and among shots of families posing with fake plastic aliens and airport-style shops he remarks to himself that "all the hopes we ever had for space travel, covered up by drink stands and t-shirt vendors. Just a recreation of what we're running from on Earth. We are world eaters." The process of space travel itself in *Ad Astra* is commonplace and uneventful, which is unlike the ways it is often treated in other science fiction media where astronauts are often shown being the first to try a given mission or to reach a new destination. Obviously, the commercialized Moon travel stands as an example, but on Roy's trip from the Moon to Mars the trip aboard the Cepheus is treated as so routine and "perfect" that the crew pass out "mood stabilizers" (via a pill shooter and zero gravity) because their human efforts are not really needed and "Lord knows SpaceCom wouldn't want you getting all emotional on us up here again." The implication is that prior missions have led SpaceCom to believe that human emotion is a liability, and it is notable that the only person who does not actually take the pill is Roy, because he has no need to stabilize his already even keel emotional state. Roy uses this opportunity, when the rest of the crew are essentially high and giddy, to review a file that Pruitt gave him about his father, confirming that he is alive and if Roy fails to contact him SpaceCom will seek to destroy the Lima Project station. This starts what appear to be the beginning cracks of Roy's unflappable nature as he flashes back to what appears to be images of himself as a child, and thoughts of his father's life.

The crew of the Cepheus receive a distress signal from a biomedical research vessel, to which the captain and Roy respond by boarding the vessel, and the captain is killed by an enraged baboon. The fallout of this event leads Roy to begin to admit in his next automated psych evaluation to emotions connected to his father. In a close-up shot of his face where he fidgets and rubs his forehead, Roy describes the futility of life, saying, "Well that's it, we go to work, we do our jobs, and then it's over. We're here and then we're gone." Karofsky and Litch remark the

> existentialist would maintain that at such moments, Roy is becoming conscious that his life is meaningless, and he is beginning to see that he has the free will to make choices that are not determined by his instincts or by his role as a soldier. (2021, 240)

Roy goes on to describe how he understands the "rage" of the baboon, saying, "I've seen that rage in my father, and I've seen that rage in me, because I'm angry they took off. He left us." Closing his eyes hard and motioning with his hands, Roy displays a great deal of emotion for the first time in *Ad Astra*, saying that "when I look at that anger, and I push it aside, just put it away, all I see is hurt." Roy is introspective and understands that hiding his true emotions keeps him "walled off" and keeps him from "really caring for someone," and he says, "I don't want to be that guy, I don't want to be my dad." *Ad Astra* has a complicated relationship to this idea of either being emotionally human or emotionally detached, given that this scene of Roy finally beginning to open up is immediately followed by a scene in which he must take command of the Cepheus to manually land it when the new captain is too emotional and scared to do so.

On Mars, Roy is tasked with sending messages to his father through "secure laser transmission," but in the beginning, he is only allowed to do so in the form of a pre-written "authorized text." Roy is put in a small soundproof room and given a letter to read from. The language in the letter is formal, and stunted, containing words like "ameliorate" and using the formal salutation "father" instead of "dad." In short, the letter is as emotionally detached as could be expected coming from SpaceCom. In between transmission sessions, Roy is put in a small "comfort" room that projects large images of nature on all the walls in an attempt to make him feel more at home. Roy cycles between these two rooms, both that "project" some form of futile connection, and appear claustrophobic and maddening for Roy. Breaking the script, Roy begins a session with the words, "Dad, I'd like to see you again." He follows this sentence with a discussion of their shared dedication to space exploration, and ends saying, "I hope we can reconnect. Your loving son, Roy." Lips trembling and fighting back tears as the transmission is sent, Roy is quickly thanked for his help and told that SpaceCom will "be returning you to Earth in short order" because his "personal connection has made you unsuited for continued service on this mission." For the first time, Roy's BPM is elevated, and is made to take an immediate psych evaluation to see if he can return to Earth, which he quickly fails. Roy is told he must go to the comfort room until he is deemed fit for travel back to Earth.

A human native of Mars, Lantos, informs Roy that the Cepheus is now being commissioned to head to Neptune and destroy Roy's father and what remains of the Lima Project. She shows him footage of Roy's father admitting to killing the rest of the Lima Project crew because they wanted to return home to Earth. This scene contains a nice connection between Rick Altman's classification of the semantics of all science fiction, that being speculative futuristic technologies, and the syntactic thematic elements of existential science fiction. Lantos hands Roy a futuristic transparent tablet to view this footage, and when his father says that "we will not turn back" and that he is "forever driven on this quest" the film cuts to a low-angle shot of Roy from beneath and through the transparent tablet, so that both Roy and his father's heads appear superimposed. Futuristic science fiction technology is being used to make an existential point about the influences and (dis)continuities of generational identity. Roy decides to secretly board the Cepheus to confront his father, and needing to approach the launch site from underwater, he travels through murky water saying, "I must accept the fact I never really knew you, nor am I you." However, much like other instances where *Ad Astra* presents a point, and then its counterpoint in the following scene, Roy's statement about not being like his father is followed by him boarding the Cepheus and accidentally killing the rest of the crew. He says he had no "hostile intent," but his actions led to the death of the Cepheus crew, much in the same way that his father killed his crew because of his believed good intentions. Aboard the Cepheus, Roy fully succumbs to the emotional connections to his father and his ex-wife through flashbacks, blaming them on "the zero G and the extended duration of the journey." He says that he always thought he would prefer this kind of solitary environment, but "must confess" that it is wearing on him "both physically and mentally." This sequence ends by crosscutting between Roy and his father's faces multiple times, and a shot of an empty captain's chair into which Roy slowly dissolves into as the Cepheus approaches Neptune. The implication of this surreal sequence is that Roy is now more like his father than he would admit, but whether this is generational influence, genetics, or the impact of deep space travel is a question that *Ad Astra* leaves open. Roy takes a capsule to go from the Cepheus to the Lima Project station, and as he passes by the rings of Neptune and thinks to himself that "in the end, the son suffers the sins of the father" a power surge strikes his capsule, serving to not so subtly actualize this statement's metaphor.

Once aboard the Lima Project station, Roy encounters his father, who is towering above him from the top of a cylindrical shaft, and tells him that he is here to stop the power surges and bring the two of them home. In a close-up on Clifford's face, he looks down on Roy and responds by saying that "this is home" and as far as Earth was concerned "there was never anything for me there, I never cared about you or your mother or any of your small ideas." The film cuts to a close-up of Roy's face, which does not move or emote when hearing these cruel statements, save for a single tear that rolls out of his unblinking eye. Clifford says that he never "once" thought about home, to which Roy responds matter of factly, "I know, Dad." Roy rises, metaphorically but also literally because of the zero gravity to meet his father face to face, and tells him he still loves him and still wants to take him home. Clifford is struggling with the fact that his life's work, the attempt to discover other forms of sentient consciousness in the universe, has failed, and hopes that the work can be continued by Roy and him together. Roy remarks that the mission, and his father, have not failed because "now we know, we're all we've got." Where Clifford sees solitude in the universe, Roy sees purpose and meaning. Karofsky and Litch connect this theme back to an "existentialist interpretation" saying that "Roy becomes aware that his life lacks objective meaning and comes to recognize that any value that his life has must be generated from him" (2021, 240). As Roy attempts to get his father and his data back to the Cepheus, Clifford uses thrusters to fling them both into space, forcing Roy to make a decision between moving on with his own life and holding onto his generational baggage. Tethered together, Clifford is literally weighing his son down, dragging him into oblivion. As they float face to face at the edge of our solar system, Clifford says, "Let me go, Roy." As Roy unclips his father, severing the literal connection between the two and symbolically letting go of the emotional baggage associated with him, he thinks to himself, "Why go on, why keep trying?" Karofsky and Litch argue,

> Sartre would maintain that Roy is the absurd hero because he does not try to avoid the choice; instead Roy makes his choice. He lets his father go. And in so doing, Roy creates his own values in a world that has no objective meaning. (2021, 241)

The screen fades to absolute black before panning back up to the light of Neptune's rings and a subsequent shot of that light bouncing off Roy's visor.

In a sense, Roy is reborn finally out of the shadow of his father. Sartre importantly notes that

> the first effect of existentialism is to make every man conscious of what he is, and to make him solely responsible for his own existence. And when we say that man is responsible for himself, we do not mean that he is responsible only for his own individuality, but that he is responsible for all men. (2007, 23)

Over shots of swirling gaseous planetary bodies, Roy remarks that his father's data showed that "beneath their sublime surfaces, there was nothing.

No love or hate. No light or dark. He could only see what was not there, and missed what was right in front of him." Roy acknowledges the journey he has gone on to now define his own existence so he can grow in his connections to others, saying, "I am looking forward to the day my solitude ends, and I am home." The psych evaluation mantra from the beginning is repeated, "I am active, and engaged. I am aware of my surroundings and those in my immediate sphere. I am attentive," but this time when he says that "I am focused on the essential, to the exclusion of all else" it is said over a shot of him waiting to meet his ex-wife at a diner. He concludes by saying, "I'm unsure of the future, but I'm not concerned. I will rely on those closest to me, and I will share their burdens, as they share mine. I will live and love. Submit." The shift in the language of reliance on those close to him significantly changes Roy's positioning within his own generational history as well as to humanity.

CONCLUSION

Juxtaposed as bookends, not because they are a definitive beginning and an end, but because they represent the trajectory of the existential science fiction media text, *Gravity* and *Ad Astra* show their connectedness and similar existential concerns. Both films feature protagonists who have suffered loss and have chosen to emotionally wall themselves off from the rest of the world, and must introspectively move on to avoid succumbing to a form of cold inhumanity. By combining somewhat solo protagonist missions, generational connections that must be explicitly dealt with, and a version of existentialism that puts primacy on defining one's existence internally as opposed to those external forces that plagued them, these films present a potent version of existential science fiction. In the case of *Gravity*, we have a film that either stands as influential at the beginning of the existential science fiction media trend or as an early and fully codified example of the trend spurred on by some other textual, industrial, or audience force. And in the case of *Ad Astra*, we see all of the same syntactic thematic elements playing out in the same manner as so many other existential science fiction media texts, speaking to the powerfulness and potential longevity of this trend going forward. The next chapter will extend most of the same ideas and threads, including generational influences on existential thoughts, by looking at *Interstellar* and *Arrival* as two media texts that fully embrace contemporary industry and audience hospitality for deep philosophical musings in the science fiction genre. They will be shown to contain their own flavor of existential exploration, namely the use of family connections to form an intergenerational continuity of identity.

Chapter 4

Interstellar, Arrival, and Continuity of Identity

After taking a deep look at the historical side of existential science fiction, and the generationally focused bookends to the current existential trend in *Gravity* (2012) and *Ad Astra* (2019), it seems appropriate to turn our attention to media that works through the philosophical concept of continuity of identity. This chapter will begin a series of chapters in this book that explores various contemporary science fiction media for the ways in which they are primarily concerned with engaging existential questions about how human beings construct and maintain their identities. Specifically, this chapter will explore two films made within three years of each other, *Interstellar* (2014) and *Arrival* (2016), that exemplify existential ruminations on life, memory, and continuity of identity. Neither film stretches the definitions of science fiction, as both involve some form of interstellar travel, with humans traveling among the stars in *Interstellar* and extraterrestrial visitors from another galaxy in *Arrival*. Their emphasis, however, is not on the antagonism present in so many other science fiction media that encounters other planets and aliens, but instead is on a deep dive into science. Bradley Schauer describes how within the science fiction genre, "depending on the historical period, different strategies have risen to prominence, including an emphasis on scientific accuracy" and "greater psychological complexity" (2016, 8). Both films exemplify the current science fiction media trend to focus on scientific fidelity and complexity, with *Interstellar* talking at length about concepts like relativity and wormholes and *Arrival* diving deep into linguistic structures and theories. The thematic commonalities between *Interstellar* and *Arrival* are also remarkable, from their reliance on memory as a way to construct our continuity of identity to their use of a circular plot where the past, present, and future can all influence each other. Both films move through cinematic time and space at a pastoral pace, emphasizing almost melodic editing cadence, aside from a few more action-heavy sequences in *Interstellar*. Both films' opening sequences mess with viewers' perception of time and memory by providing narration sequences that by films' end take on new meaning about continuity of self and characters. Both films also work to use the possibilities contained within the existential science fiction subgenre to provide characters the ability to transcend linear conceptions of space and time, through black holes in *Interstellar* and linguistics in *Arrival*.

INTERSTELLAR (2014)

With a budget of $165 million, a director whose previous films included a big-budget superhero trilogy, and a runtime of nearly three hours, it would be natural to assume that *Interstellar* would be a standard action-heavy science fiction film. However, instead these features are leveraged into a contemplative epic more about existential philosophical musings than about antagonistic villainous forces. Director Christopher Nolan describes "an interesting moment where science realizes it has to begin addressing abstractions and human elements" describing these as "things that defy easy characterization and analysis—things like love" (Jensen 2014). The scientists that were consulted to create realistic black hole imagery describe how this film was "the first Hollywood movie to attempt depicting a black hole as it would actually be seen by somebody nearby" (James et al. 2015, 1). They discuss the balance between Nolan and the visual effects supervisor's desire for accuracy and the Hollywood economic imperative, saying that while making images of the black hole's "fully realistic accretion disk" they "were committed to make the film as scientifically accurate as possible—within constraints of not confusing his mass audience unduly" (James et al. 2015, 22). Nobel Laureate and producer Kip Thorne describes how from the beginning of the film's conception he and producer Lynda Obst had two rules that stayed relatively firm: that the science in the film would not violate established laws of physics and that any speculations would come from ideas that respectable scientists would regard as possible (2014). *Interstellar* exists squarely within the Thomas Flynn–described existential (and scientific) "imaginative mode that employs art and example to bring home in concrete fashion abstract principles" (2006, 106). Containing elements such as documentary footage from *The Dust Bowl* (2012), musings about existence, time, memory, and identity, and the Dylan Thomas quote "Do not go gentle into that good night. Rage, rage against the dying of the light" as a leitmotif, *Interstellar* is not your typical Hollywood big-budget science fiction film. It also contains nary a true antagonist, beyond one sequence of a selfish astronaut, relying instead on "monolithic nature" like dust storms and tidal waves for drama (Jensen 2014). One character says that in space "we face great odds, death, but not evil," and it is through this focus on the philosophical as opposed to the oppositional that *Interstellar* comes to epitomize the contemporary existential science fiction film.

Interstellar opens with a slow moving tracking shot of literal dust falling on a bookcase and a toy space shuttle, with a narration from documentary footage that situates these moments in the past, while intercutting in the introduction of the main character, NASA pilot Tom Cooper. An older woman narrates that her "dad was a farmer . . . of course he didn't start that way," followed by a smash cut to a futuristic jet flying, something going wrong, and it is revealed to be Cooper dreaming about his traumatic crash the last time he flew. In walks Cooper's daughter, Murph, and the editing and narration heavily implies that the older woman and Murph are the same person, which ends up being true. This narrative device works to establish, much like in the case of *Arrival*, that the stakes of *Interstellar* will be about the full continuity of our lives, buttressed by our memories and the connections they can facilitate across generational lines (an echo of the previous chapter).

This sequence is followed by a montage of different interview shots of older people discussing what it was like to live during a time of dust and crop issues. If these interviews carry an air of verisimilitude, it is because other than the woman discussing her father the farmer, the rest "are interview subjects from Ken Burns and Dayton Duncan's 2012 documentary 'The Dust Bowl,' and they are speaking about their experiences in that real environmental catastrophe" (Rosenberg 2014). *Interstellar* leverages this borrowed footage to lend credence to its fictional story that revolves around a dystopian near-future Earth that has, without narrative explanation, become increasingly inhospitable to growing food. The setting looks straight out of the Great Depression, with older looking farmhouses, and a literal dust bowl as narrators from the Burns/Duncan documentary describe having to cover their mouths and noses so as to not breathe in too much. As one man describes having to set their tables with the cups and plates upside down, a shot of a laptop opening next to a dust-covered old farmhouse counter shows the past and the present side by side. The narrated documentary structure drops away for the time being, giving way to a scene with Murph trying to discuss a "ghost" in her bedroom who keeps knocking things off of her bookshelf. The documentary memories were being layered on top of one another, and then are quickly juxtaposed with the concept of the past as a ghost, which becomes a central theme of *Interstellar*. Cooper, Murph, and Tom, Cooper's teenage son, leave the farmhouse for parent-teacher conferences, only to get sidetracked by a flat tire and a drone that they see flying overhead. After chasing it by truck through a cornfield, Cooper is able to take control of the drone, let Murph land it, and then harvest it for its solar panels and internal computers. Murph wants to let the drone go, but Cooper insists that "this thing needs to learn how to adapt, Murph, like the rest of us." This theme of adapting or stagnating becomes important, as many seem to want to focus solely on the situation at hand with the lack of food, and not look toward the future. Textbooks have even been rewritten to claim that the Apollo missions were a "brilliant piece of propaganda" so as to keep people focused on Earth and not the stars above. Cooper explains to his father-in-law that the world has "forgotten who we are: explorers, pioneers, not caretakers," and crucially for the idea of existential science fiction that "we used to look up at the sky and wonder, at our place in the stars. Now we just look down and worry about our place in the dirt."

Human beings' place in the dirt is revealed to Cooper to be even more dire than assumed, when he and Murph are led to a secret government facility by coordinates sent from the ghost through gravitational manipulation of the dust. Once there, what is left of NASA explains that even the current corn crops will die out soon, but there is hope because a mysterious wormhole appeared about fifty years before the "present" of *Interstellar*, and they have secretly sent probe missions into the wormhole to find three potential extragalactic planets for human relocation or colonization. Human relocation is plan "A" and involves figuring out how to overcome gravity to get a massive space station off the ground, whereas colonization is plan "B" and involves transporting fertilized human embryos to whatever planet option is most hospitable. In either case, *Interstellar* is working through the idea of species survival as a macro continuity of identity, with one option being the literal continuity of those currently alive on Earth, and the other option being the general continuity of the human race itself. This choice is coalesced and individualized with Cooper being asked to command the "Endurance" mission to explore these three planet options, through wormhole interstellar travel, knowing that he may be giving up some or all of his time with his children. Murph is angry at his decision to go, and in an attempt to say goodbye, Cooper says that Murph's late mother once told him that "we're just here to be memories for our kids" because "once you're a parent, you're the ghost of your children's future." The idea of intergenerational continuity through memory not only reinforces that plan "A" is the ultimate goal, but also ties into the documentary interview structure of the beginning of *Interstellar*. It is also interesting to note, though completely unsurprising, that when pressed to find the existential and emotional core of these media it is often humans' connections to family, and children specifically, that is thematically most common. As was argued in the previous chapter, the semantics of science fiction, combined with the syntactic themes of connections across generations, is a powerful existential combination.

The journey to the first extragalactic planet is all about time, specifically the theory of relativity. The planet orbits close to a black hole, and the crew is told that every hour they spend there will equal seven years of time past for those on Earth. Dr. Brand says that they "need to think about time as a resource, just like oxygen and food, going down is going to cost us," which connects directly to an important tenet of existential philosophy. Thomas Flynn describes the existential "recommendation to examine and assess the life decisions that establish our temporal priorities in the first place" because "time is of the essence," a limited resource, and is "made concrete by how we handle our immersion in the everyday" (2006, 6). However, the planet turns out to contain massive waves that make it uninhabitable, kills a crew member, and water logs their return vessel, leading to twenty-three years relatively passing on Earth during their journey to the surface. Cooper, who just lost decades with his children, asks Dr. Brand if there is a way to get the time back, maybe by going into a black hole. Dr. Brand shakes her head and says, "Time is relative, okay. It can stretch and it can squeeze, but it can't run backwards . . . the only thing that can move across dimensions, like time, is gravity." Dr. Brand goes on to describe who the "they" is that opened the black hole and that they could be "beings of five dimensions" who might perceive time as "another physical dimension" that can be traversed, but says it is not possible for the crew. Cooper then watches messages from home, as he sees the continuity of his children's lives play out in a sort of mediated fast-forward. He watches his son grow up and raise a family of his own through recorded video clips over the twenty-three years. Cooper then sees his daughter, Murph, grown up and the same age as when he left Earth. *Interstellar*, at its midpoint, pulls off its own play on continuity by moving into a close-up on Murph's grainy video clip and cutting back to Earth for the first time on the click of her stopping the recording. This cut opens up the parallel story lines that occupy the rest of *Interstellar*, a father and daughter separately trying to preserve the continuity of the human race.

Whereas Cooper is singularly concerned with saving his family, and preserving as much potential future time with them, the Dr. Brand's father back on Earth (also Dr. Brand) knows that there are individual concerns and then there are the concerns of the whole of the human race. In a message to his daughter, the elder Dr. Brand, the audio of which plays over a shot of her face, says that to "confront the reality of interstellar travel, we must reach far beyond our own lifespans. We must think not of individuals, but as a species." It turns out that this Dr. Brand has been lying about the ability for plan "A" to work given the constraints of gravity, which he reveals to Murph on his deathbed. This confession is one of a series of counterposed character motivations within this segment of *Interstellar*, based around this idea of the individual/family versus the whole/humanity. Cooper wants to save and see his children, which colors his decisions. The younger Dr. Brand is secretly in love with an astronaut on one of the two remaining planets, the revelation of which causes the crew to choose the other planet to explore first. Dr.

Brand is visibly upset about this decision, and when confronted by Cooper she reminds him that if the planet they have chosen is uninhabitable then they will not have enough fuel to both explore the third planet and get home, so "you might have to decide between seeing your children again, and the future of the human race. I trust you'll be as objective then." Proving prescient, once on the second planet, they discover that the astronaut, who scouted it out, Dr. Mann, found it desolate and unable to sustain life, but he lied in his transmissions to Earth so that he might be rescued. This jeopardizes the mission to save humanity as he prioritizes his individual desire for survival. What follows is the only true antagonistic sequence of the film, as Dr. Mann defends the elder Dr. Brand's decision to lie about plan "A" by saying that "he knew how hard it would be to get people to work together to save the species instead of themselves or their children," then proceeds to prove this statement true by trying to kill Cooper, blowing up one of the other crew members, and trying to steal the Endurance ship. This somewhat villainous antagonist in *Interstellar* should not be ignored; however, he spends the entire time during these selfish deeds monologuing about how the survival instinct in human beings is too strong to be avoided.

Dr. Mann is unsuccessful in killing Cooper or stealing the Endurance, but he damages the ship enough that he leaves Cooper with no other option than to sacrifice himself (and TARS the tactical robot crew member) to give Dr. Brand the boost she needs to get to the third planet. Though the colonization plan "B" is ultimately successful through this maneuver, because of space-time relativity the mission ends up taking nearly eighty years to accomplish and lands Cooper in a black hole. The crucial reason for this plot device is revealed in this black hole, as Cooper is shown that not only can he influence the bookcase and dust in Murph's bedroom across all moments of time, but he was also always Murph's "ghost" who brought himself to this space-time moment. This black hole sequence is represented in a cinematic space referred to as a "tesseract" that resembles an infinitely traversable series of windows into Murph's room from behind the bookcase, connected by light trails (figure 4.1).

TARS tells Cooper that the "they" that brought them here "constructed this three dimensional space inside their five dimensional reality to allow you to understand it," but Cooper figures out that he and TARS are the "they" all along and that they brought themselves here to send black hole data to Murph using gravity so she can use it to make plan "A" work. Cooper's relationship with his daughter is "quantifiable," and he remembers Dr. Brand telling him that "love is the one thing we're capable of perceiving that transcends dimensions of time and space." Love is the continuity of lives capable of bridging time and space. The explanation of this "bridge" between the past and the present is intercut with scenes from Murph and Cooper's past and present, and the circular nature of this gravitational manipulation means that Cooper

Figure 4.1 Cooper Is Able to Traverse Time and Space in the Black Hole "Tesseract."
Source: *Interstellar* (2014). Screenshot taken by author.

and Murphy's memories, lives, and identities exist in a contemplative space outside of past, present, and future. It also means that Cooper and Murphy can use these memories and circular continuity of identity to reframe their own lives, which is a model of contemplation that is perhaps unique to existential science fiction. In fact, considering the ways in which time travel narratives often work under the presumption or avoidance of changes to the past, the immutable circle that *Interstellar* creates further enhances the concept of literal continuity. Both the characters of *Interstellar* and the film itself use "time as a resource, just like oxygen and food," and the result is a narrative that engages deeply with the existential turmoil that often surrounds love, lifetimes, familial relationships, and the difference between the individual and the human race. By making both time and space bendable, sometimes into a circle, sometimes compressing and stretching, concepts like love and life become more immutable, and *Interstellar* leverages time and memory in service of our continuity of identity (both as individuals and humans).

ARRIVAL (2016)

Similarly, *Arrival* is deeply interested in exploring the ways in which love can transcend the assumed characteristics of linear time, using the bond between a mother and her daughter as a constant that variables like time and space bend to accommodate. The plot revolves around twelve extraterrestrial vessels that appear around the globe, and one linguist and one physicist trying to figure out how to communicate with them. *Arrival* is structured around the linguist's life, and the apparent loss of her daughter prior to the aliens' arrival. The film is lyrical, cinematically stylized, and nearly wholly without action, aside from a brief sequence where a few soldiers sabotage a linguistics session with an explosion. The film is an adaptation of the Ted Chiang short story, "Stories of Your Life" (2002), which mostly follows the same plotline with minor changes to the way the aliens, called Heptapods, contact the humans and the way the narrative is structured as it appears as a letter from the linguist, Louise, to her daughter on the day she is born. This narrative device means that the temporal perspective of "Stories of Your Life" is very different from *Arrival*, and contains no mystery in terms of when different events in Louise's life took place. From the start of "Stories of Your Life," Louise is speaking from the perspective of someone who can see the whole continuity of her life simultaneously, a concept that *Arrival* will use as a big Hollywood-style third act reveal.

Box office receipts are not always wholly explanatory about a cultural environment, but if we compare this film to another existential science fiction film *Contact* (1997) from around twenty years prior, there are some interesting parallels and divergences. Both films are about the use of science to communicate with extraterrestrial entities, spearheaded by a female scientist with the appearances of being driven by the loss of a beloved family member, and both experiencing solo epiphanies through this communication that changes their outlook on life and humanity. At the time of release, *Contact* was said to be "cerebral and less suspense or action-oriented than the general run of big-budget summer pics" and that the film "looks to find solid mainstream audience acceptance cued by good reviews and upbeat word of mouth" (McCarthy 1997). However, the audience reception led to *Contact* only barely earning more than its budget in domestic box office receipts (Box Office Mojo, n.d.c). When *Arrival* was released it was similarly viewed as a film that "transcends the limitations that so often govern the less creative examples of the subgenre, instead using it as a loose conceptual foundation upon which to build a theoretically-informed examination of what precisely it is that makes us human" (Heller-Nicholas 2016). Perhaps speaking to a more hospitable reception environment, *Arrival* earned more than double its production budget in domestic box office receipts (Box Office Mojo, n.d.b). As idiosyncratic as it may be to compare just two films, when taken in conjunction with other existential science fiction films, like *Interstellar*, a film like *Arrival* works to address questions of humanity, memory, and life itself in a more supportive media industry environment than may have existed before.

Arrival, much like *Interstellar* with its documentary narration, begins with the layering of memory in the form of the main character, linguistic expert Louise Banks, recounting the moments that made up the life of her daughter,

Hannah, who died of an unnamed illness at age twelve. Narrated over slow moving shots of Hannah growing up and ultimately dying, Banks describes the relationship of time and memory, saying, "I used to think this was the beginning of your story. Memory is a strange thing. It doesn't work like I thought it did. We are so bound by time, by its order." The function of this narration, and specifically this last line about time and order, is designed as a misdirection for viewers who are led to assume that this opening sequence, and others intercut throughout the film, takes place in the past in respect to the primary narrative about the arrival of extraterrestrial spacecraft at twelve locations across the planet. The film even goes as far as using a language trick to imply the primary narrative happened after the death of Hannah, when Banks says, "There are days that define your story beyond your life. Like the day they arrived." The use of the word "beyond" is specifically used to imply "after," but is actually being used to literally mean beyond the borders of Hannah's life, before or after. These implied linguistic choices continue in subsequent scenes, such as when Louise is talking to her mother on the phone, and we only hear Louise's side of the conversation. Louise tells her mother that she is "about the same" and that she is "fine," with the strong implication that her mother was asking about her feelings regarding Hannah's death. Throughout the course of *Arrival*, which deals with the linguist Banks and theoretical physicist Ian Donnelly communicating with the extraterrestrials concerning the reasons for their arrival, Banks's daughter is never mentioned in the "present"-day scenes. Audiences eventually learn that the aliens, called Heptapods, actually arrived before Hannah was born, but the misdirection is clearly designed to tap into our conditioned desire to organize stories into linear narratives. *Arrival* uses this linear assumption as a counterpoint to the way the Heptapods will be shown to perceive time.

Banks is recruited by the U.S. government and armed forces to determine if the Heptapods pose a global threat, and she is tasked, along with Donnelly, to decipher their language. The Heptapods give access to their ship once every eighteen hours, and through a series of hazmat-suited, glass-barriered, and smoke-comprised language and vocabulary sessions between Banks, Donnelly, and the Heptapods, common understanding begins to develop (figure 4.2).

Audiences would be right to feel skeptical about the motivations of these alien visitors, as countless other media texts that start this way end up with some form of attack or invasion attempt. The ships' prominence in the sky is even visually reminiscent of *Independence Day* (1996). That the extraterrestrial visitors want nothing more than to teach us their language is a foreign concept in the science fiction genre. Narratively, *Arrival* is aware of this incongruity with typical science fiction fare, and so the film provides an audience surrogate in the form of Colonel Weber. He repeatedly asks Banks

Figure 4.2   Eschewing Big Action Scenes for Intergalactic and Interspecies Linguistics Lessons, *Arrival* Leverages the Science Fiction Genre in a More Cerebral Manner than Most Media of This Genre. *Source*: *Arrival* (2016). Screenshot taken by author.

to explain her strategies in communicating with the Heptapods, and expresses his concern that they may have ulterior motives. Not only does this provide a sounding board for Banks to explain complex linguistic concepts to the audience/Weber, but also serves as a commentary for any viewers (or studio executives) who might be wondering when the typical science fiction action is going to happen.

Significantly, the first word that Louise attempts to convey to the Heptapods is "human," which she writes on a whiteboard and says, "human, I'm human." The Heptapods respond by showing their cuneiform, circle-based language for the first time. There are twelve Heptapod ships around the world, with teams at every location trying to accomplish the same task, but it is this simple act of ontological declaration that elicits the first meaningful contact with the alien race. In the next session, Banks and Donnelly are able to establish the two Heptapod's names, but more importantly Banks removes her hazmat suit and begins to understand the structure of the cuneiform language itself, which propels the film toward the connection between the Hannah framing story and the Heptapods. This is marked by the first of many of what the audience perceives as flashbacks to when Hannah is alive, a blurry shot of a silhouetted young girl looking at what appears to be a horse, but turns out to be a vision of her future child. Cinematically, this reveal is shrouded by Louise's reaction after these visions, because she silently looks increasingly both distressed and upset, which would be a natural reaction to both thinking about memories of a lost child and also having memories of an unknown child pop into one's head.

What audiences are not told yet is that the Heptapod logograms language consists of nonlinear orthography that is "free of time," has "no direction," and once understood gives the user the ability to perceive across time. The more Louise understands the language, the more her ability in this regard grows, and the more she sees visions of Hannah. The film's explanation is based on the "Sapir-Whorf hypothesis, a theory of linguistic relativity that, in its strongest form, argues that language affects thought" (Zeitchik 2016). Louise describes this hypothesis as "the language you speak determines how you think," and the more she learns to "speak" Heptapod the more her visions and dreams of the future occur. Though in the linguistics field the Sapir-Whorf hypothesis has been discredited to a degree, linguist John Engle calls *Arrival* a "wonderful and timely film" that has "reopened the world of the Sapir-Whorf hypothesis to a far wider audience" and that it is "not beyond reason to surmise that language and the way their speakers think are interdependent to an extent" and "reasonable to conclude that conceptions of time are informed by the nomenclature of a culture" (2016, 99). Much like *Interstellar*, this deep exploration of scientific concepts in a major Hollywood film represents an existential "imaginative mode that employs art and example to bring home in concrete fashion abstract principles" (Flynn 2006, 106). The first clear connection between the Heptapod language and its power over time comes in a crosscut scene about Hannah trying to figure out a word. It begins in the "present" with Louise zooming in on a close-up shot of a single Heptapod cuneiform logogram while we hear Hannah from the future asking, "What's this term, here?" The scene cuts to the "future," coded as the past for audiences in a warm sepia tone, where Hannah explains that she needs to know what the "sciency" term for a competition where "both sides end up happy" is. Louise tells her that if "you want science, call your father," but as Hannah walks away her echoing footsteps pulls Louise back into the "present" where she learns from Ian both that the Heptapods have split their language gift into twelve parts and also the term "nonzero sum game." The moment she hears Ian say these words, the scene cuts back to Louise telling Hannah the term in the future. A lot is happening in this sequence, and audiences could assume that hearing Ian say "nonzero sum game" just reminded Louise of a time in the past that she thought of the same words in a conversation with her daughter, but more than likely this would be *Arrival*'s first clear indication that time and memory are relative. This sequence also connects the idea that continuity of knowledge must be achieved and that we need to work together as a species to unlock the true power of the Heptapod language.

In the penultimate session with the two Heptapods, Louise approaches the dividing glass between the two species, puts her hand up to control the cuneiform, closes her eyes, and sees her future daughter as a baby. The Heptapods release a screen-filling amount of cuneiform smoke, and what was once one instance of language becomes one-twelfth of the entirety of their language, needing to be combined with the other twelve heptapod language segments from around the world. In the final session, a Heptapod tells Louise their language is meant as a gift to "help humanity" because in "three thousand years" they will need our help. Louise asks how they can know the future, and she is given a flash of Hannah, to which she asks, "Who is this child?" The Heptapod comes right out and says, "Louise see future, weapon opens time." If there were any viewers who had not figured out the not-so-shrouded secret by now, the daughter sequences from the beginning of *Arrival* and throughout the film are now fully revealed to have been diegetically flash-forwards. After the session, she tells Donnelly that the Heptapod language is the weapon/gift because "if you learn it, when you really learn it you begin to perceive time the way that they do. So you can begin to see what's to come." Louise pieces together her future, and is now fully capable of using the language, through the idea of circular possibilities and probabilities, to see and experience any part of her life simultaneously, even future "memories (and expertise) unfolding into her brain like an involuntary Proustian memory in reverse" (Fleming and Brown 2018, 352). *Arrival* is presenting a form of time reminiscent of philosophers who grappled with concepts of free will and determinism, as well as human beings' relationship to time itself. Thomas Flynn describes existential philosophers, such as Sartre, who viewed the "possibility of possessing a desirable situation 'all at once' without having to await its necessary, temporal unfolding" as an ideal (2006, 6). Gilles Deleuze expresses a similar sentiment when arguing that ethics is nothing more than becoming "worthy of what happens to us, and thus to will and release the event, to become the offspring of one's own events, and thereby to be reborn" (1993, 149).

Despite the present-day threat by China to begin attacking the Heptapods, Louise sees herself at a future event celebrating the whole world working together in peace to understand the Heptapods language and true intentions. What follows is a crosscut sequence where Louise is shown to be able to access future knowledge in real time in the present. At the future event, she begins to speak with China's General Shang, who says that the only reason he changed his mind about attacking the Heptapods is because Louise called him on his private number. When Louise says, "I don't know your private number," Shang turns his phone to her and says, "Now you know." Shang does not understand the Heptapod language to the level that Louise does, but he tells her that he knows "it was important for you to see that," implying she will be able to access that information in the past. Back in the present, Louise steals a satellite phone, dials the number, and then pauses when Shang picks up, because she does not yet know what she needs to tell him to change his mind. Crosscutting between the present and her future conversation with Shang, Louise learns in real time that she will have repeated to Shang his wife's dying words, translated as "War doesn't make winners, only widows."

She can now view and experience the entire continuity of her life with the clarity of the simultaneous past, present, and future, much in the same way as Cooper is able to access the entirety of moments in his daughter's bedroom in *Interstellar*. Beyond the Sapir-Whorf hypothesis, *Arrival* does not spend too much time on the technicalities of how knowing Heptapod gives someone access to their entire life's continuity, but the Chiang short story version provides some more insight in this regard, describing a physics concept known as Fermat's principle, or the principle of least time. Ian describes this concept to Louise after the Heptapods reacted positively to being shown it, saying that the route any "light ray takes is always the fastest possible one" (Chiang 2002, 118). Louise struggles with the concept, later asking Donnelly to clarify because to her it "just doesn't sound like a law of physics" for light to be able to know where it is going ahead of time (Chiang 2002, 124). He tells her that light "has to examine the possible paths and compute how long each one would take" and that to do so cannot involve course corrections, but instead requires that the light does "all its computations at the very beginning" (Chiang 2002, 125). As Louise begins to understand Heptapod and its connection to Fermat's principle in "Stories of Your Life," she begins to see a world in which "one needed knowledge of the effects before the causes could be initiated" (Chiang 2002, 130). The Heptapods are teleological in their worldview, and knowing all the possibilities they "act to create the future, to enact chronology" (Chiang 2002, 137), and instead of "using language to inform, they used language to actualize" (Chiang 2002, 138). It is as if the Heptapod language gives users the superability to process all possible outcomes and events of your life, and knowing how you would respond to each. Much like light scans for the path of least time, your mind can now process the most probable future. In *Arrival*, we are shown Banks ruminating on a question she poses to Donnelly, "If you could see your whole life from start to finish, would you change things?" In the "Stories of Your Life," Louise delves even deeper into this question, saying, "Now that I know the future, I would never act contrary to that future" (Chiang 2002, 137). In both versions, despite knowing that her daughter will die, Louise chooses to experience those future memories, saying in *Arrival* that "despite knowing the journey, and where it leads, I embrace it and I welcome every moment of it."[1] The circular narrative of *Arrival* is different from *Interstellar* in its positioning of past, present, and future, but because of Louise's foreknowledge "memories" still take on a contemplative pose as they are used to develop the continuity of her identity.

CONCLUSION

The connection of circular memory, identity, and time between these two films is striking, when considered among the recent wealth of existential science fiction media that work to similarly understand our place and existence within time and space. Whereas, science fiction has always been interested in locating the human, the ordinary, within the extraordinary, and though earlier works have had their existential moments, it is significant to see a genre so dedicated to exploring our very human existence through these markers of time, space, memory, and identity. By bending time into a circle, or at the very least nonlinear, both *Interstellar* and *Arrival* connect the fabric of identity through the way our memories can define the way we perceive the past, the way we function in the present, and the way we progress toward the future. David Fleming and William Brown write that *Arrival*'s relationship to time contains a call "spiritually to come to terms with the future, which already has been, and to become worthy of events that are yet to come and yet which have already taken place," but this sentiment could apply to Cooper in the *Interstellar* black hole as by "understanding that in some senses we are dead already, we learn to appreciate life" (2018, 366).

NOTE

1. "Stories of Your Life" takes this idea to an extreme, in a way that Hollywood was never likely to adapt, having Hannah die via an apparent rock-climbing accident, which is infinitely more preventable than the incurable apparent genetic disease in *Arrival*.

Chapter 5

Annihilation and Refraction of Identity

Annihilation is a 2014 book by Jeff Vandermeer, adapted into a 2018 film written and directed by Alex Garland. The book was conceived of and written as a trilogy, with subsequent books entitled *Authority* and *Acceptance* all released in 2014, but the film only adapts the first book, *Annihilation*. Both versions of the story follow an unexplained occurrence originating at a coastline lighthouse, where the surrounding area contains many mysterious and anomalous characteristics, including a translucent border that appears to be only able to be crossed one way in but not out. In both versions, many expeditions have been sent in by a secret government division, but most have not returned, and when they do the participants do not seem like their previous selves. Both versions primarily chronicle an all-female expedition group, led by a psychologist, with the primary biologist/botanist protagonist volunteering to go into the area because their husband was one of the returnees from the previous expedition. Once inside, both book and film expeditions encounter DNA-spliced organisms, crumbling group dynamics (potentially from area contamination), evidence of violence among previous expeditions, an otherworldly entity connected to the lighthouse, and the eventual deaths of all those on the expedition except for the biologist/botanist protagonist.

This setup is rife with science fiction allegorical potential to address all kinds of existential questions and themes, such as the nature of identity over time, our place within our given environments, and how different forms of trauma can fundamentally change who we are as a person. And much like a lot of science fiction literature, the comparisons between the novel and the media adaptation are helpful in understanding these thematic and philosophical underpinnings. This comparison will also allow for an opportunity to touch on the ways in which political economic factors like studio pressures, property acquisitions, and production time lines can influence the adaptation.

Jack Boozer describes the unique connections that adaptations have with these factors, saying that

> unlike the solitary, imaginative origin of most fiction (however informed by a cultural milieu), the composition of an adapted screenplay takes place not only under the shadow of myriad narrative expectations but in a complex environment of business, industrial, and artistic considerations. (2008, 5)

Annihilation the film may have been released four years after the book, but the rights to the book trilogy's adaptation were acquired in 2013 by Paramount Pictures and Scott Rudin Productions before any of the books had been published (Fleming Jr. 2013). The screenplay for the *Annihilation* film adaptation was finished before the second and third books in the trilogy were published, and writer and director of the Alex Garland describes the process as a "freeform" adaptation where it was the "experience of reading the book that felt most relevant" not necessarily any given plot point (2018). With the permission of Vandermeer, Garland describes an "adaptation which was a memory of the book," writing the screenplay without going back and rereading the source text (2018). Garland argues that this methodology was an attempt to be faithful to what he experienced while reading, which was the "dream-like nature" of the book (2018). What this also means is that the film itself may be approaching the thematic content of refraction more explicitly, as the adaptation is refracted through the writer/director's memories, while addressing refraction in the plot of the film literally.

Taking into account all of the production time lines and economic factors, as well as the professed nature of the adaptation itself, the result is a film adaptation that takes the content of the book and through condensing and visualizing its identity thematics ends up expanding on its existential potentials. The metaphor of the border is one example: in the *Annihilation* book, the border is only hinted at expanding, whereas in the film the border is explicitly expanding and is said that it will eventually reach "cities, states, and so on."[1] The connection between the expansion of this all-encompassing, DNA-altering area and what it means for our human nature is made by writer/director Alex Garland who comes right out and says that the force in *Annihilation* has a "metaphorical element to it, a sort of unknowable expanding existential thing" (Bishop 2018). There are many other instances where Garland takes the heart of what exists in the book version and moves it to the forefront of the film's thesis about our identities being an ever-shifting constellation of the things that have happened to us, the people and places we carry with us, and the people we wish we were compared to how others see us. I am not arguing that the film is some form of "cliffs notes" version of the plot, though it might be argued that all film adaptations condense in some manner, but that the film is itself a refracted version where the existential themes of the book become concentrated and focused. Instead of a prism refraction of light, a visual theme that the film version leans on heavily, this is a magnifying glass refraction of light, and audiences are the ants on the sidewalk.

ANNIHILATION (2014)

Classifying *Annihilation* as science fiction does not initially seem like a stretch, given the reliance on potential extraterrestrial forces, but when pressure is put on the details of the story it has some science fiction gaps that need explaining. The science and technology is not overtly futuristic or counterfactual, especially given the purposeful reliance on older technologies in Area X. There are mentions of cell phones that resemble ours, which places the time period as roughly contemporary, though the discussions of government agencies like "Central" and events do not place the books within any of our known time lines. Where we can lay claim to these books as science fiction, or certainly speculative fiction, is that its "objective is to explore, to discover, to learn, by means of projection, extrapolation, analogue, hypothesis-and-paper-experimentation, something about the nature of the universe, of man, of 'reality'" (Merril 2017, 27). *Annihilation* works to try and define our existence through the refractory nature of the unknown phenomenon of Area X.

Voice becomes one of the primary ways in which characters' identities and thoughts are refracted, as readers are often given mediated versions of experiences through journals, videotaped interviews, hypnotized phone calls where we are given the "scrubbed" version. The entirety of *Annihilation* is told through the first-person perspective of the biologist as if the words appear in a field journal she is leaving behind in Area X. From the start of the book, the most prevalent idea is that Area X itself changes everything that enters it, and there is deep concern about what would happen if that phenomenon spread. The borders of Area X are not depicted as technologically impenetrable as they are in the film, though the idea of potential contamination extends to these devices to the point that those at the Southern Reach facility are concerned that transmissions that originate from Area X could themselves be a contaminating force. This means that instead of radios and transmissions not working to and from the area, like in the film adaptation, these types of technologies are not given to those on expeditions, not because they would not work, but because there was a rule that they were to "attempt no outside contact, for fear of some irrevocable contamination" (Vandermeer 2014, 6). What enters Area X can no longer be trusted to be the same if it were to ever come out. This idea of one's identity being different inside

Area X is highlighted, as those on expeditions were "discouraged from using names" because they "belonged to where we had come from, not to who we were while embedded in Area X" (Vandermeer 2014, 7). It is also theorized that Area X itself will react to certain stimuli more than others, and because the phenomenon is not fully understood this was to be avoided. So those at Southern Reach felt that stripping of names, "making people into their functions," would not "trigger Area X's defenses" (Vandermeer 2014, 389). The issue is that no one at Southern Reach truly knew what triggered Area X, or what that meant if it was triggered. Most times those who entered never came back out, and when they did they were not the same. The first expedition produced the only potential survivor who might still be himself, a man named Lowry, but if the defense trigger theory was correct it is possible that Area X did not initially recognize the expeditions as threats and adjusted accordingly for future teams. Others that returned would be shells of their former selves who claim to have not seen anything out of the ordinary, despite their journals and other evidence to the contrary. They would turn out to be doppelgängers who had all the original's memories that Area X created and sent back into our side of the boundary. They were copies of the original identities, refracted through what Area X had learned about them while inside.

A further layer of refracted identity and purpose, that becomes a primary pseudoscientific mechanism in the whole *Southern Reach Trilogy*, is a detailed version of hypnosis that the psychologist performs on the rest of the expedition team, bordering on mind control. She has conditioned the team with trigger words and phrases to literally not see the reality of some elements in Area X, such as the true nature of "the tower," which is an inverted version of a lighthouse that goes subterranean instead of being built up like a normal tower. The psychologist uses the phrase "*Consolidation of authority*" to convince those on the expedition when they descended the tower that they would "continue to see a structure that is made of coquina and stone" despite it being a living breathing organism in reality (Vandermeer 2014, 22; emphasis in original). The crux of a good portion of *Annihilation* is about whether or not we can use our environment and experiences, symbolized by the main character becoming inoculated to the hypnosis by literally breathing in part of the tower, to resist outside influences and truly understand the world around us. This breathing in of golden spores in the tower creates a growing "brightness" in the biologist, leading to her eventual survival in Area X and her finding her true purpose and reason for going in the first place.

Initially, the biologist describes her reasons for going into Area X as her "existence in the world has become" empty and having "nothing left to anchor me, I *needed* (Emphasis in original) to be here" (Vandermeer 2014, 9). The survivors of the preceding expedition had included the biologist's husband, and they all appeared in their homes suddenly after a year's absence, much like the main character Lena's husband does in the film. He was distant and unlike his former self, much like others who returned from Area X, but in the case of his expedition team all the survivors died from systemic cancer within six months making a clear carcinogenic connection to Area X. The biologist's husband remarked in a taped interview after returning that he felt as if he was "walking forever on the path from the border to base camp" and that the "trees are not trees the birds are not birds and I am not me but just something that has been walking for a very long time" (Vandermeer 2014, 55). It is revealed that the husband is correct, because as a doppelgänger copy he is not the same version, and so when readers find out that the real husband asked the biologist before leaving "Will you come after me if I don't come back? If you can?" her true motivations for going to Area X become clear (Vandermeer 2014, 125). She knew it was not her husband who came out, knew that it was a refracted version who emerged, so she went in to find the real him or what had happened to him.

The refraction does not just occur upon exiting Area X, as even within the refraction of identity is omnipresent. The biologist discovers a pile of journals from previous expeditions in the lighthouse, one of which is her husband's, and her reaction includes a musing about the changing of everything in Area X, saying the "sparrow that shot up into the blue sky one morning might transform mid-flight into an osprey the next. This was the way of things here" (Vandermeer 2014, 73). However, in the same reflection on the journals she notes the ways in which all of life imposes these types of changes, saying, "The madness of the world tries to colonize you: from the outside in, forcing you to live in its reality" (Vandermeer 2014, 72). Both of these thoughts, the way Area X changes everything and that the outside world does the same, work through the idea that we all change who we are throughout the course of our lives. However, the psychologist presents a different view, one that will be highlighted in the film adaptation, when the biologist tries to fight against the idea that she is changing because of Area X. The psychologist says, "Of course you're not. You're just becoming more of what you've always been. And I'm not changing, either. None of us are changing" (Vandermeer 2014, 85).

Whether we self-actualize some latent version of ourselves or we imbue ourselves with our experiences and environments over time are two sides to an existential question that *Annihilation* seems poised to address given its medium and genre. Reading her husband's journal, the biologist is presented with another complication on this existential question, what happens when we are confronted with our past self? The journal describes the husband actually seeing the doppelgänger versions of himself and his expedition group walking into the tower, and he remarked,

> We were dead. We were ghosts roaming a haunted landscape, and although we didn't know it, people lived normal lives here, everything was as it should be

here . . . but we couldn't see it through the veil, the interference. (Vandermeer 2014, 110)

The implication is that when we change, or become more of who we always were, we do not notice the changes, because they are gradual and slight. The biologist makes the connection to this gradual change through her memories, which she says "are real and not real" and that "I remake them in my mind with every new thought, every remembered detail, and each time they are slightly different" (Vandermeer 2014, 125). In the film and in *Acceptance*, it will be made clear that time expands in Area X, where a few weeks in the outside world equates to years inside, concretizing the allegorical and condensed nature of change and refraction of identity in *Annihilation*, as what would normally be experienced as a lifetime of changes occurs in a short time period.

Perhaps, it is appropriate that so many of these elements will become condensed and embellished in the film adaptation, including the origins of the Area X phenomenon. In the final pages of *Annihilation*, the biologist finally addresses and theorizes about this origin, saying,

> Think of it as a thorn, perhaps, a long, thick thorn so large it is buried deep in the side of the world. Injecting itself into the world. Emanating from this giant thorn is an endless, perhaps automatic, need to assimilate and to mimic. . . . It created out of our ecosystem a new world, whose processes and aims are utterly alien— one that works through extreme acts of mirroring, and by remaining hidden in so many other ways, all without surrendering the foundations of its *otherness* as it becomes what it encounters. (Vandermeer 2014, 126; emphasis in original)

The perspective of a sole expedition member would be expanded upon in subsequent books in the trilogy, and there would eventually be similar connections made, but comparing this version of *Annihilation* and the film adaptation, which addresses this origin in the very first shot, tells us a lot about different media and different ways of addressing existential questions of identity.

ANNIHILATION (2018)

Much has been made about the ways in which it is appropriate to compare a work of literary fiction to its visual media adaptation. Fidelity to the source material is always a topic among audiences and early literary critics, but a shift in the way the adaptation has been analyzed for its own merits and properties is important for this chapter. Most recent scholars, such as Robert Stam, agree to defocus on fidelity, especially as "an exclusive methodological principle," both because "it is questionable whether strict fidelity is even possible" and a recognition that "an adaptation is automatically different and original due to the change of medium" (2000, 55). Stam also notes the strict adherence to fidelity assumes and "reinscribes the axiomatic superiority of literary art to film" (2000, 58). In fact, the relationship between the two, the way they refract each other, is the way this chapter will treat each version. André Bazin describes a version of film criticism that would, with some distance, view adaptation in the lens of "the unity of the work of art" where a book and its filmed adaptation as "equal in the eyes of the critic" (MacCabe 2011, 6). Colin MacCabe argues that this conception views adaptations as not able to "be understood as one medium translating another but as two media making a whole that was not reducible to the sum of its parts" (2011, 5–6). It is not as if one cannot be understood without the other, just that with their relatively concurrent production/writing schedules, and the ways the film teases out themes from the book, the two exist able to enhance one another. From a methodological perspective, this means focusing on moments in the film that may not be directly adapted from the book, but share the thematic existential spirit of the source material. So much of what occurs and is seen in *Annihilation* the film is not in *Annihilation* the book, but writer/director Alex Garland believes in the inherent connections regardless of simple fidelity. When describing things that are different in the film, he says that "ultimately, if you keep going down the evolutionary chain, it comes from the book, because the book is the source material, and it doesn't matter if it's in the book or not; that's sort of the genesis of it" (Bishop 2018).

For example, from the very first moment of *Annihilation*, the film, the condensing difference is seen when a meteor-like object is shown careening toward Earth and crashing into a lighthouse. In the third book of the *Southern Reach Trilogy*, it is revealed that Area X is caused by a small "organism" that came "remote from Earth" and ended up embedded in "the glass of a lighthouse lens" (Vandermeer 2014, 555), but this fact would not have been known by Garland, assuming he is telling the truth about never having read past *Annihilation*. In this instance, the idea of Area X being extraterrestrial was an implied part of the book's DNA, now refracted through the adapted film version. This meteor crash is followed by a close-up of red-morphing material and cutting to a shot of a cell dividing under a microscope. The theme of cellular change, shifting at a molecular identity level, is made evident, as Lena begins lecturing over the microscope slide, saying, "This is a cell. Like all cells, it is born from an existing cell and by extension all cells were ultimately born from one cell. A single organism, alone on planet Earth, perhaps alone in the universe." The connections between all cellular division in the universe and the way the lighthouse organism will begin to take over everything in its path is continued as Lena tells a class of students that it is "the rhythm of the dividing pair, which becomes the structure of every microbe, blade of grass, sea creature, land creature, and human. The structure of every thing that lives, and everything that dies."

Annihilation works fast to establish this cellular change theme, even before entering the anomaly area, with metaphors of painting rooms and many shots of reflective surfaces. Lena's husband Kane appears in their home after a yearlong absence where he was presumed dead, and when Lena questions him he claims to have no idea where he was or how he got home. A close-up shot of the two holding hands across the kitchen table hints at the refraction of Kane's identity, as their hands are shown through a glass of water. Their relationship and their identities are mediated, refracted by the water. Kane takes a drink from the glass, says he does not feel well, puts it back on the table, and a close-up of blood swirling in the water further deepens this connection of body, DNA, and identity mixing. They are both taken to a facility called Area X because the actual anomaly area is called the Shimmer in the film adaptation, where Kane is being monitored and Lena is being recruited. Lena sees Kane through glass and hooked up to a ventilator, and flashes back to a conversation with him before he left for the Shimmer. They are discussing God, and Lena extends the cellular theme by explaining,

> You take a cell, circumvent the Hayflick limit, you can prevent senescence. It means the cell doesn't grow old, it becomes immortal. Keeps dividing, doesn't die. We see aging as a natural process, but it's actually a fault in our genes.

The Shimmer itself is refractory in nature, as the boundary gives the appearance of a moving translucent oil slick rainbow, or maybe a child's bubbles on a flat surface, and the space within the Shimmer also has a hazy look as if through a prism. The film's psychologist, Dr. Ventress, describes it as "a religious event, an extraterrestrial event, a higher dimension" but ultimately says that there are "many theories, few facts." What they do know is that it started three years prior at the lighthouse, it looks like a shimmering boundary wall, that the area is increasingly expanding, and that nothing they send in comes back out. The border itself is an interesting idea, as both the book and the film are cagey about how it functions. Something about crossing into the border is either physically or mentally problematic for expeditions, as in the book the team is hypnotized into not remembering crossing, and in the film they are shown crossing into the Shimmer and waking up four days later having set up camp and eaten rations, without remembering anything. This is part of the way time is refracted within the Shimmer as Lena later will describe being inside for only days or weeks, while she is told she has been inside for four months. In the book, the border is heavily guarded, and the only known entrance/exit is controlled by a gate, but the question of whether one could freely physically cross back and forth is not fully answered. Similarly, in the film, it is said that expedition teams do not come back, but when Lena's team is in the Shimmer no one actually tries to go back through the border. Characters often talk about doing so, threatening in both the book and the film to end the mission and head back to the border, but something always convinces them not to do so. It is possible if they tried to leave they would also be physically unable, but it is the mental impediments that speak to the idea that who we are changing into is a process that is itself immutable once begun.

Time is refracted, air and light are refracted, and animal and plant life itself is refracted at a cellular DNA level. Lena remarks that multiple different plants are "growing from the same branch structure . . . like they're stuck in a continuous mutation." Cassie is attacked by something under the water, and when it emerges it appears to be a normal alligator, albeit an albino one. However, upon examination after killing the alligator, it appeared to have sharklike teeth inside its mouth, to which Lena remarks that "something here is making giant waves in the gene pool." There seems to be an intensifying feature of the Shimmer, as Lena says that "the mutations were subtle at first, more extreme as we grew closer to the lighthouse, corruptions of form, duplicates of form" which she calls "echoes." The team eventually comes across plant mutations that are in the shape of humans, resembling freestanding topiaries that Lena remarks have "grown this way." When a team member named Anya says that "doesn't make any sense," the team's physicist, Josie, gets to the heart of what *Annihilation* is trying to say about the refraction of identity. She describes the hazy light, saying, "The light waves aren't blocked, they're refracted," and she hypothesizes that if you sequenced the topiary plant genes you would find "human hox genes," the genes that define the body plan. Josie makes the connection that the book was working through explicit, saying, "the Shimmer is a prism, but it refracts everything" including "all DNA." When Josie later asks Lena if she thinks the refraction theory is correct, Lena confirms that she "checked my blood last night, it's in me." Josie then reveals to Lena that her arm has plants growing through it, and says that she does not want to face or fight this Shimmer refraction, implying she wants to succumb to it. What follow are shots of Lena chasing an increasingly plantlike Josie, increasingly visually obscured by the other plants, only to have Lena come upon a field of more topiary humans, knowing that one of them is now Josie.

As the group's mental state begins to break down because of the refracted DNA processing inside them, Anya notices a physical manifestation, saying, "When I look at my hands, and my fingerprints, I can see them moving," meaning that she is literally shifting her identity markers within the Shimmer. There is a similar moment that precedes this fingerprint discussion, where the expedition group comes across a video from the previous expedition, where Kane cuts into the stomach of a still-living expedition member only to reveal that his intestines are moving and contracting in his abdomen like a coiling snake. Here, and with the fingerprints shifting, the existential thesis of *Annihilation* is laid bare, that our literal identities are always ever-shifting. The Shimmer just exacerbates the situation by making the process physical and viewable. After Anya is killed by the bear who also killed Cassie, and can now mimic her vocal cries for help, Dr. Ventress says that their movement toward the lighthouse must restart immediately because she fears that "the person that started this journey won't be the person that ends it." They know that they are changing, through the Shimmer, through their previous traumas, and through the people around them, and they are attempting to futilely hold onto a version of themselves that may not exist anymore. Everyone and everything that goes into the Shimmer is refracted, but *Annihilation* is making the argument that we are all the refracted results of our lives and environments.

Perhaps the most important and straightforward scene in the film that explicitly makes connections between what the Shimmer is and the characters that have decided to cross its border happens earlier when Lena and Cassie are rowing across a lake. During this quiet moment, Cassie asks Lena what kind of past "do you carry around her neck" because there "had to be something" given that "volunteering for this is not exactly something you do if your life is in perfect harmony." She goes on to describe how they "are all damaged goods here," listing addiction, self-harm, and the loss of a child to leukemia as reasons to go on this seemingly hopeless mission. Cassie makes the link explicit, saying that she, and potentially everyone on this mission, is suffering "two bereavements, my beautiful girl and the person I once was." Loss is argued to be its own refractory force on our identities.

Lena seems to lie about her motivations for going into the Shimmer, telling Cassie that her husband had been killed in action, but later revelations in the film, notably whether she knew that the Kane that showed up in her home was actually her husband, potentially point to the truth in her statement to Cassie. The version of Kane who showed up at Lena's home and held her hand is revealed to be a refracted imposter through a video recording of Kane killing himself with a phosphorous grenade, only to have another Kane step out from behind the camera into frame. The question, which is never answered, is whether Lena always knew that it was not her husband who came out of the Shimmer, and instead was motivated to go in as a potential rescue of the "real" Kane (or at the very least a confirmation of what happened to him). This motivation is implicitly stated in the book as well, and the existential refracted identity connection can be made that our loved ones will change, and we are as much responsible for the stewardship of their continued identity as they are themselves.

The term "annihilation" serves as a major titular theme in this regard, both in the book and the film but in different ways. It is actually said out loud in both versions, and both near the end of the story when the biologist/Lena confronts the psychologist/Dr. Ventress at the lighthouse. In the book, the word "annihilation" is said as a further hypnotic cue to try and get the biologist to commit involuntary suicide, whereas in the film Dr. Ventress says it as she dies. She tells Lena that "it's inside me now," "it's not like us, it's unlike us," "it will grow until it encompasses everything," "our bodies and our minds will be fragmented into their smallest parts until not one part remains, annihilation" at which point a billow of smoky, fiery, oil slick material begins spouting from her mouth until her body disintegrates into cellular light particles. The director, Garland, says *Annihilation* is "about the nature of self-destruction in a literal sense: cells have life cycles and stars have life cycles and plants and the universe and us. You, me, everyone. But also psychological forms of self-destruction" (Bishop 2018).

Lena goes into the lighthouse and goes down into a hole that looks like it could have been caused by the meteor. A mass appears that is ever changing and forming, looking like a light and sinew kaleidoscope, and in an extreme close-up of Lena's eye it pulls a drop of blood through her skin and into the mass. Once the mass has her DNA, it divides and replicates into a shimmery, metallic-looking, version of Lena that mirrors her movements in what appears to be an attempt to learn how to be Lena. At the moment the replication appears complete, when the shimmery metallic surface gives way to an exact copy of Lena, the "real" Lena tricks the replicated version into holding a phosphorus grenade, destroying the copy along with the lighthouse. This appears to set off a chain reaction, where because the mass mirrored and refracted the flames and the source burned, so too did the Shimmer and all the refracted DNA in the surrounding area. The pathological cancer metaphor of the shifting mass is obvious and is borne out many times throughout the film, such as when the team discovers the deceased body of a previous expedition team member, and his body has become a grotesque spore and coral-like tapestry that is literally embedded in the wall of an abandoned pool. The book also leans heavily on the idea of Area X as carcinogenic to human cells, given that the versions of the "11th" expedition team that came back all died from systemic cancer. However, the metaphor of cellular change and shifting bodies is not monolithic given the ways the film, and the book, work to establish new identities through these cellular changes. In the aftermath of the fire, Lena is being interrogated by a member of Area X, and when he says that the entity was destroying everything, Lena responds by saying, "It wasn't destroying, it was changing everything, it was making something new." Lena is not the same Lena that went into the Shimmer, both literally and figuratively, much the same as none of us are the same versions of ourselves over time. The film ends with Lena coming in to see what she knows is a replicated version of Kane. She confronts him by asking, "You aren't Kane, are you?" He responds by saying, "I don't think so," and asking if she is Lena. Though she does not respond, they embrace and both of their irises are shown to glow in the same manner, implying that though the Shimmer is gone that part of their identities continues to be refracted through its source.

AUTHORITY AND *ACCEPTANCE* (2014), BRIEFLY

Much of what can be said about the subsequent novels in the *Southern Reach Trilogy* coalesces the arguments made in this chapter; the medium of the novel affords a different version of thematic presentation. Perhaps more nuanced, perhaps deeper, but certainly different. That the series was conceived of as a trilogy from the start, and the three books were all written in the course of one year, it is no surprise that Vandermeer would use the breadth of the books to bring out the existential themes of *Annihilation*.

Refraction is still an implicit theme throughout the second and third books, explicitly worked through in the *Annihilation* film adaptation, but is explicitly addressed in *Authority*. Unlike in the film, however, this discussion of refraction is symbolically evoked through the description of the lighthouse beacon. Originally, the beacon was manufactured overseas, "shipped over just prior to the states dissolving into civil war," and first resided in an older lighthouse on a nearby island (Vandermeer 2014, 320). Containing "more than two thousand separate lenses and prisms," the bulb's light "was reflected and refracted by the lenses and prisms to be cast seaward" (Vandermeer 2014, 320). Great care is taken to describe this light refraction, saying that the "'light characteristics' could be manipulated in almost every conceivable way. Bent, straightened, sent bouncing off surfaces in a recursive loop so that it never reached the outside" (Vandermeer 2014, 320). Light, its refracting beacon, and the lighthouse itself as a magnetic force for expeditions combine to form the symbolic metaphor of the *Southern Reach Trilogy*. Put in existential terms, as humans we are projects and that "existing as an individual is always dynamic and underway, never static and complete" (Flynn 2006, 25). In *Acceptance*, this metaphor becomes explicit, as it is theorized that "bodies could be beacons too" and the idea of how different people handle their own light is compared to the lighthouse:

> A lighthouse was a fixed beacon for a fixed purpose; a person was a moving one. But people still emanated light in their way, still shone across the miles as a warning, an invitation, or even just a static signal. People opened up so they became a brightness, or they went dark. They turned their light

inward sometimes, so you couldn't see it, because they had no other choice. (Vandermeer 2014, 399)

Area X physically, and symbolically, condenses the process by which we take on our experiences and environments, the light, and we refract those factors through our identities, the lighthouse beacon. Science fiction is often theorized to use "allegory as a productive way to deal with contemporary issues without attracting unwanted scrutiny" (Schauer 2016, 59), though here the beacon is used allegorically to explain the unknowable Area X and its influence on the identity of anything that enters. Literary critics have linked the *Southern Reach Trilogy* in this regard to the concept of the "hyperobject," which is a term that includes things like black holes and is used "to describe events or systems or processes that are too complex, too massively distributed across space and time, for humans to get a grip on" (Tompkins 2014). Area X is a hyperobject that characters and readers find too big to understand or explain fully.

The closest the *Southern Reach Trilogy* comes to trying to truly explain the Area X phenomenon is in the repeated discussion of the term "terroir." Described as "all the physical elements of a place that can affect the character of wine made from it" (Steiman 2014), terroir is allegorized and theorized throughout *Authority* and *Acceptance* as the reason for Area X's particular characteristics. Whitby, Southern Reach's resident holistic environments expert, brings this theory to Control, saying it is the "idea that Area X could have formed nowhere else" (Vandermeer 2014, 218). The theory is then extended to be a way to understand a given person by the specific environment they exist in, as Control tries to look through all of the documents, notes, and even dining receipts of the former director "trying to build a true terroir vision of the director—her motivations and knowledge base—from everything he was sorting through" (Vandermeer 2014, 232). Though Control claims to have eventually come to the conclusion that the terroir theory "began to fall apart" when scrutinized (Vandermeer 2014, 232), he continues to take Whitby's terroir notebook everywhere including into Area X itself when he enters with the biologist at the end of *Authority*. There is never a definitive affirmation of this idea of terroir, but given the way Vandermeer uses it as a structural thematic framework, the assumption can be made that the way the extraterrestrial object mimics, a point made explicit in the film adaptation, would lead to terroir being the most likely explanation.

The way the trilogy finally ends is just as shrouded in subtlety and inconclusiveness, as none of the remaining characters' fates are fully explained. Control walks through the light at the bottom of the tower, appears to overload Area X, and may have destroyed or neutralized it somehow. The biologist copy, called Ghost Bird, and the assistant director of Area X proceed to walk out from the tower throwing rocks in front of them to see if they ever encounter the border, but readers are not given an answer if they ever do. Finally, the last page is a letter from the psychologist to the lighthouse keeper that is just about the ways in which people can get caught up with the world and in the wrong situations, speaking specifically about the keeper's role in the creation of Area X, but that it is not their fault and that acceptance is a way to move past denial. The implication is that the whole trilogy is about the things that define us over time, and the ways in which we might be able to use our newly refracted identities to find some form of truth or dignity. This sentiment is echoed by literary critic Joshua Rothman connecting the idea of the hyperobject to "glimpses of a whole that's, by its nature, unknowable" but that there is "dignity of the search for even partial truth" (2015).

CONCLUSION

We can use the career of Alex Garland as a microcosm of the ways in which the existential science fiction media text has grown into an "imaginative mode that employs art and example to bring home in concrete fashion abstract principles" (Flynn 2006, 106). Starting his career as a writer for *28 Days Later* (2002), he first wrote a screenplay for a science fiction film with 2007's *Sunshine*, which weaves some minimal existential elements such as species survival into a story about the sun dying. However, the bulk of the story follows a pretty simple antagonist/protagonist action structure. Growing as a screenwriter, Garland wrote and directed *Ex Machina* (2014), which deals deeply with existential questions of identity and consciousness and presents a more subtle and nuanced version of dramatic good versus evil. Finally, Garland wrote and directed *Annihilation*, which this chapter argues is primarily about questions of refracted identity, and contains no actual antagonist beyond a force of (extraterrestrial) nature that is not evil but simply mimics what is in front of it. The development and production environment had evolved in its hospitality to media texts that eschewed action for existential inquiry, parallel to Garland's evolution as a filmmaker in the same regard. This does not mean that Hollywood is some utopic haven for cerebral films about philosophical ideas, just that there are cracks in a more monolithic action science fiction model. As a counterpoint to the utopia idea, perhaps it is telling that despite the ways in which the film takes the implicit themes of the novel and makes them more explicit and condensed, the head of Skydance Productions, a co-financer of *Annihilation* with Paramount, thought the film was "too intellectual" and "too complicated," and asked for changes including making the main protagonist "more sympathetic as well as tweaking the ending" (Kit 2017). These changes were ultimately rejected, as the person who had final cut privileges, Scott Rudin, believed in the director's vision, but the studio responded by flexing their power and making "a deal with Netflix to take over the international distribution of the film" they "deemed to have certain box office ceilings" (Kit 2017).

I think that admitting to my consumption experiences with these "two media making a whole" in the creation of "the unity of the work of art" is somewhat illustrative of how they work together in concert (MacCabe 2011, 5–6). I first saw the *Annihilation* film in theaters when it was initially released, having known nothing of the sourcebook (let alone the trilogy). Then, for this chapter's research and writing, I initially rewatched the film, then read the sourcebook, then watched the film one more time. The reason I think this is important is that the different versions of this story of an area of coastline beset by some unknown phenomenon were all refracted in my mind. In some ways, the film became a "paratext" that could proffer "proper interpretations" for the book itself (Gray 2010, 81), much in the opposite way that reading a book before an adaptation influences expectations of the visual media version. Thematically, this meant that I saw the definitively refracted DNA of the expedition team in the Shimmer before I read it alluded to in the book. It meant I saw the shimmery advancing border and hazy rainbow air of the area inside before I read allusions and theories of the border in the book. It also meant that the film proffered its own existential interpretations of all of these moments, and the idea of ever-shifting identities that are refracted through all our lived experiences was made front and center for me long before I read the rest of the *Southern Reach Trilogy*. In some ways, this is what science fiction can do for existential questions, acting as paratexts that proffer interpretations of the real world, whether through allegory or confrontation.

NOTE

1. In the subsequent novels, the border's expansion is attributed to the delusions of the former Area X director, but then confirmed in *Authority* as it expands quickly all at once.

Chapter 6

Legion and Fractured Identity

Legion is a television show that aired on the FX Network for three seasons from 2017 to 2019. The show was designed as a tangential X-Men cinematic universe tie-in without, at least for the majority of its run, the same characters that moviegoers had been conditioned to expect with Fox's run of *X-Men* films (2000–2020), such as Wolverine, Magento, Professor X, and Mystique. Instead, the show revolved around a lesser-known protagonist/antagonist/antihero David Haller, aka Legion, and other characters that only resembled comic book characters, such as David's love interest Sydney Barrett who can temporarily trade bodies with anyone she touches much like comic book and film character Rogue can temporarily assume another mutant's powers through touch. *Legion* writer and showrunner Noah Hawley describes these tangential connections as crucial to the show's unique appeal, saying that "with the X-Men comics, there are a lot of alt universes, so that has allowed me some leeway" and that "it's a sort of origin story for David, but none of the other characters that I've surrounded him with are from the comics. It's sort of an invented world." (Holloway 2017).

This decision to make *Legion* more invented than adapted is crucial to the way it presents itself to audiences, because the leeway Hawley describes is not just in the source material but also cinematic, narrative structure, and even genre leeway that would likely not be possible in a series that was required to be more concerned with the brand continuity and marketing tie-ins associated with blockbuster characters like Wolverine. Even down to the title sequence, *Legion* is certainly a part of the same big-budget superhero universe, but it manifests these connections in a more subtle way. For the first season, in every episode the word "LEGION" appears as just letters, but then an "X" fades into the center of the "O" connecting the show to the classic Xavier's School for Gifted Youngsters X-Men logo. It is not as if unabashed superhero media cannot tackle complex material, just that the subtle nature of *Legion* gives the series more of an opportunity to engage with existential questions without the distractions of well-known characters or plotlines. *Legion* leverages its subject matter and its genre into a series that performs a deep dive into questions of consciousness, existence, and above all else identity, placing it squarely within the definition of an existentially focused narrative.

Simply asking questions about human existence is not the only criteria to being considered an existential media text. Thomas Flynn describes existentialism as a philosophical movement that often uses "an imaginative mode that employs art and example to bring home in concrete fashion abstract principles" (2006, 106). *Legion* is foundationally based on using a hyper-stylized televisual style to concretize abstract ideas and concepts. *Legion* is also, importantly, connected to Flynn's argument that it is a "defining feature of existentialist thought and method that they carry an ontological significance as well" (2006, 7). The very essence of *Legion* is about the nature of being, of identity, and what makes us who we are. Is it our memories, our perspectives, our thoughts, or none of the above? These are big questions for a superhero television show, but Amanda Lagerkvist, whose discussion of the existential nature of the digital age will be crucial in the discussion of existential science fiction video games, describes how important existential themes can be for any media to tackle big life questions. Lagerkvist argues that "the existential is evident in the concerns of representational media across history" and it is essential to "enable sense-making in relation to the precariousness of life and the basics of 'why are we here'" (2017, 98). *Legion* is, perhaps, one of the most complicated television series ever made, and uses the sense-making scaffolding of science fiction to ask these existential questions while maintaining the plausible nature of the impossible in its genre.

Although complicated in its genre-specificity, with elements of fantasy and clear literal integration in the superhero genre, *Legion* is also very much a science fiction television show. Perhaps, this is helped by the specific superhero(es) it is based on, the X-Men broadly and Legion specifically, which have always highlighted the science in superheroes. Instead of telling the story of a character like Batman, whose abilities are wholly within the realm of possible science (with the help of billions of dollars), X-Men is about human individuals, known as "mutants," who are born with superhuman genetic abilities, as a form of human evolution, such as telepathy, telekinesis, shape-shifting, regenerative health, super speed, and even weather manipulation. John Trushell describes how "X-titles, including *The Uncanny X-Men*, *X-Factor*, and *X-Force*," especially in the bronze age of comic books, "drew upon contemporary sophisticated and unsophisticated science fiction materials" and "traced themes that had become standard in science fiction stories of the 1950s and popularized through television in the

1960s" (2004, 158–159). *Legion* comes right out and makes this connection between mutant abilities and the science fiction genre, when in chapter sixteen a flashback is shown where a mutant named Fukyama being recruited into a government agency is told "there are listeners, watches, creatures from science fiction, telepaths who can read our mind."

The science in the X-Men superhero fiction is used to create a dichotomy of identity: humans versus mutants. Trushell argues that the "reorientation of *New X-Men* from superheroic soap-opera toward source science fiction also re-established the original theme of the X-Men insofar as homo superior was re-emphasised as the unhappy outcast from the oppressive society of homo sapiens" (2004, 161). *Legion* uses this split as a way not only to examine the individual identities of its characters, who have felt outcast because of their abilities, but also to explore how group identities form, split, and re-form. Jean Phinney describes this dual identity concern, positing that "at the individual level, identity formation involves the development of both personal identity and group identity" (2000, 28). Important for *Legion*, because of the ways that enemies often become allies and group identities are made fluid through individual motivations, Phinney argues that "identity development, is based on a universal need to define oneself in one's context" and that "societal norms and the historical moment set the limits for individual choice; they make some identity choices easy and others virtually impossible" (2000, 30). The group's goals, which often in this show revolve around either ruling the world/existence or saving the world from those who would rule it, set limits on the individual's identity, and those who oppose are outcast.

Legion leverages this idea of the person who is outcast because of their science fiction level genetic abilities, and takes it to its logical next step where mutants suffer existential and psychological issues because of these abilities. Summerland, a facility designed to cultivate mutants abilities, is based around the idea that mutants would be made to feel as if they were psychologically imbalanced when their abilities began to manifest, but that this was just society's inability to understand. *Legion* complicates this Summerland process by giving them a mutant who is both maligned by society because of their abilities and also has actual mental issues. When Sydney Barrett was brought to Summerland, she was able to see that her diagnosed antisocial behavior of not wanting to ever be touched was just a natural consequence of her body swapping mutant ability. However, when Summerland brings in David Haller, whose mutant name in the comic books is Legion, the question that arises is what would happen if one of the most powerful mutants was not mentally stable? Often, villains in media are portrayed as having some form of psychosis or mental imbalance, but Legion is more nuanced as he is portrayed in the comic books as suffering from dissociative identity disorder, with each identity/personality able to manifest their own mutant abilities.

David was the son of Charles Xavier, Professor X, a powerful telepath in his own right, which along with some childhood trauma led him to develop into an "Omega Level Mutant" meaning that his "dominant power is deemed to register—or reach—an undefinable limit of that power's specific classification" (Hickman 2019). In *Legion*, David is a powerful telepathic and telekinetic mutant, but his mind has been occupied by a parasitic entity since he was a baby so his identity stretched and fractured to the point of developing issues that Summerland could not explain away as societal misunderstanding.

A *LEGION* OF FRACTURED IDENTITIES

As a result of this series structure and setup, *Legion* comes to audiences untethered by elements of conventional storytelling. Unreliable narrators and events, extra-diegetic lectures about mental conditions, extremely stylized aesthetics, and astral plane rap battles are just some of the ways in which viewers are put off balance. Despite being purportedly set in the 1970s and its fervent dedication to retro chic styling of this same time period, *Legion* is narratively contemporary in its complexity and focus on the existential.[1] *Legion* is, at its core, about the various ways in which consciousness is manifested and identity is formed through its maintenance. William Lycan describes consciousness as having "to do with the internals or subjective character of experience, paradigmatically sensory experience" (1996, 1), and *Legion* spends the bulk of its narrative time in one or another inner space of a character's consciousness, whether in memories or in astral plane mental projections. Lycan examines inner consciousness through Locke and Kant's respective "internal sense" and "inner sense," saying that "consciousness is a perceptionlike second-order representing of our own psychological states and events" (1996, 13). The complexity of *Legion*'s exploration of these psychological states, events, and illnesses are only possible through representations of the inner consciousness. This show is extremely complicated, intentionally surreal, and narratively splintered, so any attempt to fully describe every character, connected plot points, and consciousness time lines would be futile in this format (and would take up far too much space). Basically, if you have not seen *Legion*, I will try to make this as simple and painless as possible. However, it will be helpful to work through some individual characters in an attempt to explore how much this show relies on fractured identities as its central theme.

First, and foremost, there is David Haller, the titular Legion, whose mutant name refers to his comic book persona's many fractured personalities. In the comic books, David suffers from dissociative identity disorder (formerly known as multiple personality disorder) brought on by the childhood trauma of watching terrorists kill his stepfather. This disorder is leveraged with genetic mutant powers passed on from his father, Charles Xavier, and David is able to absorb and develop powers for many personalities. In *Legion*, the backstory is further complicated by initially only having David diagnosed with paranoid schizophrenia, which he learns later is the result of a parasitic entity known as the Shadow King, who is actually a powerful mutant with telepathic powers named Amahl Farouk, occupying his mind since he was a young child. Farouk is one of the only other characters in *Legion* that is adapted straight from Marvel comic books. He is often depicted as a nemesis of Professor X, which *Legion* fully ties in during its third season, but in this show he is more concerned with immortality and power as he occupies different bodies and minds on his quest to find his original body. The thirty-three-year occupation of David's mind, along with his own unexplained powers, take a toll on him and his adopted family. All of these factors eventually leads David to attempt to commit suicide, which lands him in Clockworks Psychiatric Hospital where he meets Sydney Barrett whom he falls in love with.

Sydney Barrett's abilities to temporarily swap bodies through skin-to-skin touch were mentioned already, but noting the ways in which this ability develops and what it does to Sydney's identity are important to explore. When Sydney's consciousness occupies the person whose body she touched, she is also essentially occupying their mind too, so she is able to see their memories and thoughts to an extent. After the switch is over, the consciousnesses do not switch back over physical space, but instead the bodies resume their original forms. Because this ability is involuntary, she wears gloves all the time and refuses to come in actual contact with any other human being, which is treated as an antisocial behavior. The fact that David meets Syd at the Clockworks Psychiatric Hospital speaks to the mental toll this ability has taken on Syd throughout her life. She remarks about her own physical body in episode three, saying, "It's not my body, you know, it's just how I've come to think about it, if anyone can just come and go." Sydney justifies any sadness this might create by saying she has proof the "soul" exists and that she is more than just her body. For Sydney, that knowledge is helpful, but this ability contains a problematic manifestation for the person who swaps with Syd as they are potentially unaware of what is happening, such as when she intentionally swapped bodies with her mother when she was a teenager so that she could have sex with her mother's boyfriend, but the swap wore off before it was over and the boyfriend was sent to prison. This temporary nature of the body/identity swap allows for Sydney to experience not only another person's life and perspective but also the abilities of the touched person. This most closely aligns Syd with the established X-Men character Rogue, and *Legion* shows off the power of this ability when David surprises Sydney by kissing her in the first episode of the series. Sydney, in David's body, cannot control his body's powers, and accidentally kills fellow patient Lenore Busker, while David, in Sydney's body, is ushered to safety outside of the facility before swapping back and looking like himself again.

Speaking of Lenore Busker, her role in *Legion*, and its exploration of identity within the series, does not end with her death in episode one, as she becomes a part of David's psyche used by the Shadow King. Lenny, as she is most often referred to, torments David by retroactively replacing herself into David's memories before they even met, and in episode six/seven trapping everyone in an astral plane version of Clockworks Psychiatric Hospital. If Lenny's sole function for the rest of the series was relegated to being a memory of David's leveraged against him in his fight against the Shadow King, then it would not be as interesting from an identity perspective, but Lenny decides that she wants a body of her own. But even if she found a body to occupy, would it actually be "Lenny" who was reborn or some other conscious entity. Bethan Benwell and Elizabeth Stokoe speak to a split in the idea of what makes a person who they are, describing how "essentialist theories locate identity 'inside' persons, as a product of minds, cognition, the psyche, or socialisation practices" whereas "constructionist theories treat the term 'identity' itself as a socially constructed category: it is whatever people agree it to be in any given historical and cultural context" (2006, 10). *Legion* uses Lenny's new body search as a commentary on consciousness, and who we actually are as people. When David asks her in chapter ten whether she is "Lenny at all from the hospital . . . or is this just a mask," he is told, "Does it matter? Bodies and minds, humanity . . . my associate is who she needs to be at this moment." With the help of Amahl Farouk and a character named Oliver Bird whose body he was occupying at the time, Lenny is eventually successfully reborn into the body of David's sister, Amy Haller. The show leaves open the question of whether this version of Lenny is actually the same entity as the person who was with David at Clockworks, or just her memories placed in Amy's body by Farouk.

In the first season of *Legion*, the dueling forces of Division 3, the government-run force to track mutants down, and Summerland are introduced and pitted against one another over David. The leader of Summerland, a psychiatrist named Melanie Bird, who functions much like Charles Xavier does at his School for Gifted Youngsters in the comics, eventually has additional motivations for helping David that touch on *Legion*'s theme of fractured identities. Melanie's husband, Oliver Bird, who has the same type of psychic powers as David, has been trapped in the astral plane for twenty-one years, because once "he found a place where he could rule, be the creator" then he "started spending more and more time there" and "then one day he just didn't wake up." When David meets Oliver in episode four he describes the astral plane as "no place, where every day is the same, where you can imagine yourself" anything "but nothing is ever real." Oliver's real body is in a refrigerated room at Summerland, encased in a retro diver's suit. Once David develops the ability to travel to the astral plane, Melanie enlists his help to try and wake her husband up and bring him back into the real world.

Within Summerland, there are a few other recurring characters that function to enhance *Legion*'s focus on the existential nature of fractured identities. Cary and Kerry Loudermilk are two (one) characters who share an identity, with Kerry having been born inside of Cary. Kerry can come out of Cary and become corporeal, which is also the only time period that Kerry ages. Early in *Legion*, Kerry would come out as a skilled assassin who retreated into Cary when boring things happened like eating and sleeping. In essence, Kerry and Cary share an identity, but not personalities. When separated, their bond remains strong, as Cary is shown to know what Kerry is doing when she is on missions; he even mimics her fighting moves in a lab and feels when she gets shot in episode four. These characters are also not based on any particular Marvel comic book characters, but do share similarities to other fictional comic book characters. Most notably, DC Comics created a set of characters known as Firestorm, a hero who starts as Ronnie Raymond and Martin Stein being fused together in one body, though Firestorm has included multiple other people and identities over the years.

Ptonomy Wallace is a mutant who performs "memory work" at Summerland, which allows him to access a person's memories with such fidelity that he can recreate them as living experiences. In episode two, Melanie describes him as a "memory artist" and he can put anyone into any point in their lives. Ptonomy warns not to interact with the people in the memories, because though it cannot change the past it can change your memory of the past. Ptonomy tells David that it is "the museum of you" and that "it's your place you're the boss," asking him, "Where do you want to go, what do you want to see?" Ptonomy has been successful in the past helping other mutants recreate and understand their memories, though with David the memories are more complicated because his mind is shared with the Shadow King. Though David's "memory work" is fraught with danger, Ptonomy's powerful ability eventually gives David insight into the creation of astral planes, like the one that Oliver is in, where "psychic projections create a simulated reality" that looks and feels as genuine as our own reality. This astral plane projection becomes one of the central ways in which characters and identities develop in the series, with David, Oliver, Farouk, and Charles Xavier having the ability to create them, as well as Sydney, Melanie, and Lenny spending a good deal of time in them.

The characters of *Legion* provide a backdrop of identity exploration that is, at all times, fractured. From David's diagnosis of schizophrenia that is at once real and simultaneously a product of his mind cohabitation to Sydney's literal switching of identities whenever she touches someone, and every Kerry/Cary split in between, no one is wholly and solely themselves throughout the entirety of the series. Amy is Lenny, Lenny is Benny, Benny is Farouk, Farouk is Oliver, and Oliver is the espresso machine. How anyone could have a consistent version of themselves in this kind of fractured mental environment seems impossible; however, throughout the series, *Legion* still makes paramount the idea that who we are still matters.

CONTINUITY OF IDENTITY IN A FRACTURED WORLD

Legion hypothesizes that existence is consciousness, and consciousness is fractured through memories as well as the forming/changing of identity, which makes the cultivation and maintenance of a continuity of self all-important. Anouk Smeekes and Maykel Verkuyten discuss how

> humans are faced with the issue of maintaining self-continuity because they not only are aware of the passage of chronological time but also have a sense of self. Self-continuity refers to having a sense of connection between one's past, present, and future self. (2015, 165)

The characters of *Legion* must constantly work to maintain their sense of self-continuity, because this continuity is repeatedly challenged. These challenges represent an ever-shifting foundation of identity, but Smeekes and Verkuyten note that "self-continuity does not imply the absence of change but involves a conceptual thread that is established and maintained against a backdrop of constant change" (2015, 165). For instance, in the season one finale, the forces of Summerland are attempting to rid David of the Shadow King parasite for good, but when the process appears to be killing him Sydney breaks into the room and kisses him. This skin-to-skin contact sets off a chain of consciousness/body swapping that sends the Shadow King from David's body, to Sydney's, to Kerry's. Then, when Sydney, in David's body, literally faces off in a hallway against the Shadow King, in Kerry's body, the resulting clash expels the Shadow King into a bodiless black cloud. Floating along the hallway, the cloud happens upon Oliver and it attaches itself to his body. Within one sequence, the same consciousness, which is itself the two separate entities Amahl Farouk and the Shadow King, has been inside four bodies, pointing to the idea that *Legion* is primarily concerned with the fracturing of identity. On top of all of that swapping, Lenny tells Sydney earlier in the episode in the astral plane that "we're connected kid" because she had previously swapped bodies with David and that she, the Shadow King, would always be a part of her. This idea of residual connection means all of the bodies that the consciousness moves through in this season finale sequence would never truly know if they were fully and solely themselves.

One way in which the concept of self-continuity is explored and stretched within *Legion* is through the aforementioned group dynamics at play within the series. Smeekes and Verkuyten use the concept of "collective self-continuity" to refer "to the feeling that being a group member connects one's past, present, and future self" and that "the part of the self that is derived from group membership has temporal endurance" (2015, 166). Early in the series, the most important group membership seems to be mutant or human, such as is the case with Division 3's members sacrificing everything to protect humanity from mutants, aligning *Legion* with many X-Men narratives. However, as the series progresses, other group memberships, such as Summerland or David's eventual commune, become even more important to the individual characters, and by the end of the series it is the common goals of the group above individual needs that take precedence. Sydney begins the series staying at Summerland only to help David, with the ultimate goal of running away with him to live out a quiet existence on a farm. By the end of the series, she has abandoned that goal to become a leader willing to sacrifice her relationship and future with David for the good of mankind itself. Throughout season two, she appears to David from the future, and steers him toward actions that seem counter to their goals, helping Farouk get his body back, but are ultimately about the collective self-continuity of Summerland and humanity itself. David makes a similar decision by the end of the series, forgoing his very consciousness for the good of humanity.

I would not consider *Legion* to be a particularly nostalgic show, despite its clear retro chic styling from the 1960s and 1970s, because the characters do not consistently demonstrate a longing to return to some kind of past or past state. Many of their pasts are something they are trying to escape, because of previous issues with their mutant powers, not something they are trying to recreate or reinhabit. The concept of nostalgia as longing to return might not be as applicable, but Janelle Wilson works through the idea of nostalgia as a way to use the past to frame our thinking about ourselves in our development of our self-continuity (2006). Characters in *Legion* are made to consistently remember and reengage with their pasts as a way to understand their present selves, such as David having to come to terms with his misconceptions about his mind-parasite controlled memories. For example, in chapter twelve, a flashback loop of Sydney's childhood is shown to David, where she grapples with the problem of not being truly able to connect with other humans because of her involuntary touch-based abilities, even her mother. The flashback loop begins at a house party where Sydney tries on guests' coast in front of a mirror, mimicking and trying to work through her own identity crisis by trying on different people's clothes/personas. The loop then flashes to her dressing in punk garb in front of the same mirror and purposefully going to a music club mosh pit where her identity/consciousness is swapped from body to body on the dance floor. Next the loop jumps to her purposefully swapping bodies with a bully so she can beat up girls who torment her, and then finally to the aforementioned sexual encounter with her mother's boyfriend. Wilson discussed the unifying characteristic of remembering as an "active reconstruction of the past—active selection of what to remember and how to remember it" where the goal is to view the past as a "comparison to the present" (2005, 25). So though this looping trip down memory lane is not nostalgic for Sydney, she is showing David these things to teach him a lesson. We can use Wilson's views on the "act of recollection and reminiscence, and the experience of nostalgia" as a heuristic way to discuss how reliving memories "may facilitate the kind of coherence, consistency, and sense of identity that each of us so desperately needs" (2005, 8). The lesson that David learns from Sydney's tortured past is not to fix the past or get over the things that hurt us, but that "it's about the damage itself, and how it makes us strong, not weak."

One area of *Legion*'s deep reflection on identity, consciousness, and psychological processes is in the aforementioned extra-diegetic lectures about mental conditions.[2] Show creator Noah Hawley describes these lectures as "educational segments," and he introduced them in the second season to try and move from the season one idea of "individual mental illness" to a "greater idea of mental illness" where "the idea of our shared reality being a choice that we make" can lead to moments where "societies go a little bit crazy" (Wigler 2018). These sequences are narrated by a noncharacter voice, are mostly on a stark white background, and are about "trying to explain and visualize what is a delusion" (Wigler 2018). From the first sequence, in the first season two episode, they are also always about identity, as the tale of Zhuang Zhou and the butterfly is visualized. Zhuang Zhou is a Chinese philosopher who is shown having fallen asleep one day and so vividly dreamt about being a butterfly that "no longer remembered he was Zhuang Zhou" until he awoke, "but in that moment he didn't know, was he Zhuang Zhou who had dreamt he was a butterfly or a butterfly who was dreaming that he was Zhuang Zhou?" This idea of reality as a subjective, never truly knowable, experience is a common theme throughout *Legion*, as characters must consistently try to figure out whether what they are seeing, hearing, and feeling is actually happening or part of some individual or shared delusion. In the chapter fifteen educational segment, the narrator describes the lengths our minds can go to shape our own realities, saying, "We don't believe what we see, we see what we believe, and when we are stressed or our beliefs are challenged, when we feel threatened, the ideas we have can become irrational." The narrator connects this irrational turn to a central *Legion* theme, that under the pressures of society, memories, and existence itself the "human mind struggles to maintain its identity." Smeekes and Verkuyten argue that "self-continuity is often taken for granted but can be challenged by life transitions . . . and societal changes" (2015, 175).

If season one was "about looking at individual mental illness" and season two was "about the greater idea of mental illness" (Hawley, qtd. in Wigler 2018), then season three is about the ways in which our memories, mental states, and thereby our identities can change over time. We all have ideas about ourselves, our pasts, and who we have become, and sometimes that mental version of ourselves does not line up with what others see over time. In the season three premiere, the episode cold opens to a mutant named Switch hanging upside down, listening to what sounds like a self-help recording entitled "Lessons in Time Travel," which states that

> all past is future. When going back in time, remember—the present is not just a date, it's a feeling. Feel no shame about the past, no anxiety about the future. Every negative can be changed to positive once you know how.

David ruined his relationship with Sydney when after she decided in the season two finale that he would end the world with his powers he tricked her mind into forgetting this fact. David tells one of his other personalities that he did this because he "can fix it" he "just needs time," however, the memory wipe essentially functions as an amnesia roofy when David has sex with Sydney under these circumstances. This action is tantamount to sexual assault given the mind trick false pretenses, and it spurs the plot of the third season where David recruits Switch to work toward the goal of going back in time and erasing these events and choices. Through this narrative arc, *Legion* aligns closely with an introspective existentialist mentality where "the value and meaning of each temporal dimension of lived time is a function of our attitudes and choices" (Flynn 2006, 5). Thomas Flynn argues that to be an existentialist is "to examine and assess the life decisions that establish our temporal priorities in the first place" (2006, 6). David thinks that by changing the events of his past he can change his identity from villain to hero, but Sydney reminds him that he will have still committed the acts, she just would not know that he did. David must learn another existentialist lesson, that our lived time is "made concrete by how we handle our immersion in the everyday," or the present (Flynn 2006, 6).

Legion does not present its characters as wanting to live in the past or the future, but learn from them, saying in chapter twenty that "nostalgia is your enemy" but that there is also "no perfect future, time is not a river, time is a jungle filled with monsters." David's plan is to learn from his potential future, and his past demons, and go back increasingly further into his past to fix his present self. In season three, episode three, the narrative arc revolves around David, using a newly amplified Switch to travel back in time to when his parents were courting in a mental institution, but the journey creates a rift that bounces David around between before and after he was born eventually releasing "time eaters" who threaten the whole fabric of time itself.

To attempt to fix the rift, and attack the time eaters, Farouk takes Clark and Kerry to "the time between time" that cinematically functions like the 1962 Chris Marker experimental short film, *La Jetée*, in that the sequences are composed of grainy still images. Farouk says they have come here because the time eaters "have no advantage here" and are able to successfully kill one of them. This same episode shows Syd confronted by a younger version of herself as they discuss whether the future version is inevitable or malleable, as well as Lenny experiences snippets of the entire life cycle of her in utero child from birth to death, forcing her to face her unaging nature at her elderly child's deathbed. All of these sequences and events, David trying with futility to fix his present self, Farouk trying to find a place outside of time's influence, Lenny at her child's deathbed, and Syd comparing the potentials and inevitabilities of life, point to *Legion* grappling with deep existential questions about how our identity develops over time. As the episode ends, older Syd's face is repeatedly transposed with younger Syd, as she asks, "What am I?," crosscut with David telepathically lighting a time eater on fire by sheer will of his godlike powers. Time is a force upon our identities, but how that force exerts itself on us is an open question for *Legion*, as Hawley describes that the "nature versus nurture question is yet to be resolved" (Wigler 2019).

Two competing viewpoints on time's influence on our identities are presented in the series finale, as David teams up in the past with his father, Charles Xavier, to attempt to stop Farouk from ever inhabiting himself as a baby. After a montage of David through the years, the text "Lessons in Time Travel: Chapter Zero" appear, and this time it is David narrating as he both states that "who we were does not dictate who we will be, but often it's a pretty good indication" as well as the somewhat contradictory statement "if we don't believe in change, then we don't believe in time." The series may say that it does not have the answer to this split in the question of time's influence, but does pick a side in terms of what lessons the characters learn. David, Charles, and ultimately a future version of Farouk are able to convince Farouk in the past to never occupy David's mind as a baby, which has the effect of essentially erasing the versions of *Legion*'s characters we have been following, because their time lines will never come to be. In this way, David accepts that though he changes the past, it cannot help his present self, and actually erases his existing consciousness in the process. Talk about using existential themes in representational media to foster "sense-making in relation to the precariousness of life" in its viewers (Lagerkvist 2017, 98).

CONCLUSION

No one is who they appear to be in *Legion*, at least not solely who they appear to be. Everyone is something else, often buried in their consciousness beneath their physical appearance. In episode twenty-four, David tells Farouk, "You can't stop us," and when questioned who "us" is, he responds, "me." Sure, this is because David's mutant name is Legion, and he has many internal versions of himself, connected to his source material comic book personalities. However, the "us" also seems to refer to the very fractured nature of human existence and identity. Who we are as children is different from who we are as adults, and who we are to certain people in our lives is different than who we are to others. This multiplicity of existence is a central theme for *Legion*, extending well beyond its titular character.

The way a series begins and ends, assuming of course that the creators had some say in the timing of the ending, can often say a lot about its central messages or themes. Bookending the same conversation at the beginning and ending of *Seinfeld* (1989–1998), despite the very different settings, showed the trivial nature of this show about "nothing." For *Legion*, the series begins and ends with David as a baby, even using the same shot down into a yellow crib with baby David looking directly into the camera.[3] In the series premiere, this shot is followed by a montage of similarly composed shots of David as he grows up into the troubled and powerful man who will have the potential to destroy the world. In the series finale's final moments, the shot of the baby is preceded by adult Sydney and David standing over the crib, having just successfully reset the time line so that the Shadow King will never inhabit David's mind, and Sydney warning David in the show's final line of dialogue to "be a good boy." In both instances of the shot, they invoke the idea of the potential identities, personalities, and events of a person's life inherent in them just being born. *Legion* seems to be commenting on the fractured nature of identity and existence with this ending, where our potentials collapse into the singular entity that we eventually become, but that this identity is not fixed nor determined at any given point.

NOTES

1. There are a few anachronistic references, such as a mention of the Internet and a character who sings a song from the 1990s, but the overall stylings, technology, and established X-Men character time lines line up with the show being set in the 1970s.

2. These sequences are mostly extra-diegetic, as some never connect directly back to the primary narrative, and the characters do not appear to be aware they are going on, but there are some moments of connection and crossover into the diegesis.

3. A frame-by-frame comparison of the two shots shows that they are not literally the same shot, but likely different pieces of the same footage of the exact same baby.

Chapter 7

Westworld and the Embellished Remake

There are many ways to engage with remakes, from their economic considerations to audience demographics to their comparisons to their originals. Many contemporary scholars have looked at remakes from these varied perspectives, such as those who "sought to understand cinematic remaking as an industrial, textual, and critical category" (Verevis 2017, 267), and those that have written about the ways in which remakes can represent embellished versions of their originals as well as what epistemological positioning they ask their audiences to occupy (Lizardi 2010, 2014). However, for the purposes of this chapter on the existential underpinnings of *Westworld* (1973) and its television remake, the notions of embellishment and epistemological positioning seem most useful, for the level to which a remake asks its viewers to bring knowledge of the original and how they contrast philosophically. This chapter will compare the *Westworld* film with its *Westworld* television series remake to show that not only is there no epistemological reckoning in the remake series for those that have not seen the original film but also there are medium, cultural, audience, and industrial reasons that the remake series is significantly more existential than the original film. Both versions of *Westworld* contain the "android as the next step in our human evolution" theme that is so prolific in science fiction media, but it is only in the remake that this idea is truly explored.

WESTWORLD (1973)

Written and directed by Michael Crichton, *Westworld* is released during a historical and industrial era that was certainly capable of producing complex philosophical interrogations of the human condition, including within the same science fiction genre as was discussed in chapter 3. *Westworld* is about a futuristic world where artificial intelligence and android development has progressed far enough that a company named Delos has created a series of theme parks, Western World, Medieval World, and Roman World, where wealthy guests can immerse themselves in fantasies that look and feel authentic. Larry Alan Busk argues that this film interrogates the "ontological and normative status of 'reality' as opposed to illusion under the ubiquity of the virtual, the limits of ideology critique in the era of simulation, and the implications of increasingly 'spectacular' social relations" (2016, 26). This sounds complex, but it is not as existential as it sounds, with Busk positing that this serves to illuminate the "problems that confront a critical analysis of capitalist society" (2016, 26). Allegorical in nature, much like other films of the same era like *Dawn of the Dead* (1978), Busk shows how *Westworld* is "not so much an immersion into the world alleged as an immersion into the glossy caricature of these worlds as seen in Hollywood films" (2016, 28). Important for Busk, and for this chapter's analysis of the perspective of the film versus the series, *Westworld* the film starts with a commercial for the Delos parks, marking its critique as one of an economic and capitalistic nature.

Opening on a crowded airport with a stream of people filing through a corridor, the camera pans to a news reporter delivering a segment about Delos. The reporter says he is coming to audiences from Delos "again" and mentions that as "we've always said, Delos is the vacation of the future, today," which clearly marks this footage as promotional. However, the sequence also aims to create verisimilitude in the minds of filmgoers, as there are no titles or credits yet to signify this is a film, beyond the MGM logo that precedes the scene. This cold open cinematic device brings the perspective directly into the "real" world, literally just as passengers are returning from their trip to Delos, and is detached from the parks in a manner of perspective that is not achieved in the remake series until the second episode (or even the third season depending if you define it as an area fully outside of Delos). This idea of perspective becomes the most important difference between the existential exploration of the original film and the remake series, as the original centers the perspective and audience identification almost solely through the experiences of the guests, while the remake series centers the perspective at least equally between the experiences of the guests and the androids. The only shots from the literal perspective of the androids throughout the film are from the POV of the "Gunslinger" and appear as heavily pixelated views that cannot be mistaken for human vision. But this difference goes beyond POV shots, as the *Westworld* series itself does not rely on those to convey identification and connections to the "hosts." The film also never gives us a narrative window into the perspectives of the androids and what they are capable of thinking and feeling.

Instead, they appear as automatons, with clear characteristics, and "tells" that they are not human. In the Delos airport commercial, one of the guests remarks, "I think they were robots. I mean, I know they were robots," and the chief supervisor of the androids later argues that "we aren't dealing with ordinary machines here, these are highly complicated pieces of equipment. Almost as complicated as living organisms." Calling it an example of Baudrillard's pure "simulacrum," Busk says that the Westworld guests' "inability to distinguish between factitious representation and genuine article is a non-issue because *the representation refers to no genuine article*" (2016, 31; emphasis in original). However, these statements by guests and android supervisors, as well as the connections to Baudrillard, belie the fact that there are ways to immediately tell the difference between human and machine. The most notable is described by one of *Westworld*'s two main protagonists, John Blane, who remarks how humanlike they look "except the hand, they haven't perfected the hand yet." This tell proves itself out in a close-up of the android hotel bellman's hand upon arrival, and serves as a foolproof marker of the difference between human and robot. Later in the film, a Westworld worker asks the other main protagonist, Peter Martin, to "Show me your hands" as a human authenticity test.

Being able to tell the difference would seem to destroy the illusion of the Delos parks, but Busk argues it is a comfort to guests and viewers, saying that the "Delos amusement park poses a threat and becomes a catastrophe only when its promise of authenticity is fulfilled. As the guests, we wanted to experience an authentic reality—but in a controlled and disinfected way" (2016, 34). The orientation process that John and Peter go through stresses both the danger and the control in a delicate balance, both saying that guests will be able to "relive the excitement and stresses of pioneer life to the fullest" but also that "nothing can go wrong." John reiterates to Peter that "it may look rough, but it's still just a resort" and that there are safety measures in place. High body temperature sensing guns are just one of the fail-safes that differentiate human and android; however, when failure rates among the hosts begin to spread like a computer virus they become dangerous to the guests. When this illusion of control is broken, the human reaction is one of incredulity, as demonstrated by John when he is actually bit by an android snake he cries out, "That's not supposed to happen!," in a tone befitting actual fear for the first time. It is only when the illusion of control is lost, and the hosts can do authentic things that humans can do, like pose a threat to guests, that the film's critique becomes clear. The androids are simply now "acting *as they would in real life*" and demonstrating the "constitutive instability of the capitalist system" as the "insulated, protected, and predictable world they have invested in ceases to function in the desired and expected way" (Busk 2016, 32; emphasis in original). So when the hosts go on a full-on murderous rampage in Roman World, killing guests indiscriminately, the commentary of the film seems connected more to the commercial nature of the Delos parks than the potential humanity of their android hosts, which has a great deal to do with the lack of identification and perspective afforded these characters in the film.

The only time this perspective line is crossed, with the introduction of point-of-views shots from the eyes of the resident Western World villainous android, the Gunslinger, deserves more attention for the ways in which it does or does not humanize the hosts. The Gunslinger is described as being a more advanced android than the others, with specific emphasis on his advanced infrared vision. However, instead of using these advanced features to demonstrate the Gunslinger's closer proximity to humanity, it is used to widen the gap between human and android. The point-of-view shots are shown with big, blocky pixels that resemble getting very close to a cathode ray tube television, and though it allows the Gunslinger to track humans efficiently, it cannot help but appear inferior, and inhuman, from a pure vision standpoint to viewers of the film. The pixelated, infrared perspective that was touted as more advanced in the Gunslinger ends up being its downfall, as the android is unable to discern between Peter and flaming torches in Medieval World, lending weight to the idea that the *Westworld* film considers androids to be inferior to humans despite their technological advantages. Busk notes that *Westworld* embodies hyperreality in that experiencing it "may destroy the ability to experience any reality whatsoever" and that when Peter is confronted with a final encounter with an android that he mistakes for a human (even after the park's safe facade has been destroyed) that it functions as a "recognition that the pervasiveness of dissimulation may have permanently disintegrated his sense of reality" (2016, 35). This may be true for Peter, however, for audiences there can be no doubt as to which characters we are to recognize as existentially real, a point which will become much more complicated in the remake television series. The ways in which *Westworld*'s (1973) thematic critique is levied is much more on the side of the park itself and what it represents about systemic societal concerns, and not as much concerned with the relative humanity of the androids.

A brief note about the *Westworld* sequel, *Futureworld* (1976) is warranted here, not because it significantly extends the existential exploration of the original, but because it does not. Following a pair of journalists invited to the reopening of Delos' parks, with Western World swapped out for Futureworld, the plot becomes about swapping powerful humans with clones that will work to keep Delos open. The closest the film comes to any complex interrogation of existence is when the android park manager, Duffy, says the duplicates are not "mere robots, they are not machines. They are living beings, produced by the genetic information in your own cells. There are no mechanical parts.

Even those of us who created them can't tell the original from the duplicate." However, this description aligns the duplicates more with clones than androids, and the reason for their creation is more in line with capitalistic domination than existential equivalency. The film ends with the journalists besting their duplicate counterparts and proving their humanity to each other by kissing, because as one of them says, "Some things you just can't fake." This reestablishment of human dominance and authenticity blunts any amount of latent existential humanity critique contained within. The Delos parks, from their commercials to their commodification of vice, and their destruction, serve a narrative about the illusion of control over a system. The remake series will be shown to take the same semantic elements of hosts, control, destruction, and weaves in different syntactic themes of identity, reality, humanity, and existence itself.

WESTWORLD TELEVISION SERIES

Medium differences are important to understand, as there is a big difference between the level of complexity possible in two hours of cinematic content and almost thirty hours, and growing, of televisual content. Jason Mittel works through some of the reasons for television narrative complexity, especially from the late 1990s onward, connecting industrial and cultural reasons for the rise in complexity. First, Mittel describes "the changing perception of the medium's legitimacy and its resulting appeal to creators" as a "major influence on the rise of narrative complexity on contemporary television" (2015, 31). Mittel presents previous "obstacles to complex storytelling" saying that the "commercial television industry in the United States has historically avoided risks in search of economic stability, embracing a strategy of limitation," especially in an attempt to protect syndication (2015, 32). It might also be argued that some of these imposed limitations on complexity would have also been a factor across media, leading to a tendency toward safe products, and Gunslingers who do not question their existence. Mittel notes other television medium limitations on complexity, such as advertising time structures and the extension of the narrative as the primary goal, but notes that what really "opened up storytelling innovations was the recalibration of industry expectations of what a hit series looked like," such as dedicated niche audience appeal and brand image (2015, 34). Noting other technological changes and reception environments, Mittel presents a compelling argument that television's recent increasing "narrative complexity is predicated on specific facets of storytelling that seem uniquely suited to the television series structure apart from film and literature and that distinguish it from conventional modes of episodic and serial forms" (2015, 18). *Westworld*, the series, exists in a completely different medium, industrial, commercial, and cultural environment than its original source film, and it shows in the level of existential narrative complexity that is shown on the small screen.

Perhaps the most stark difference between the *Westworld* film and its television series remake is the narrative weight and perspective of the hosts' experiences. As noted, in *Westworld*, the film, the only subjective host moments come in the pixelated viewpoint of the Gunslinger, but in the *Westworld* series the primary narrative viewpoints come from the hosts, with the most notable exceptions early on being William/Man in Black and park cocreator Robert Ford. First images and words of any media can set the tone for the whole, as the commercial sequence in the *Westworld* film does. The first thing we see in the *Westworld* series, beyond the credit sequence which will be discussed in detail, is an android named Dolores sitting alone in a chair as a disembodied voice asks her if she knows where she is. She is told she is in a dream, and can wake up if she answers some questions like "Do you ever question the nature of your reality?" and "Tell us what you think of your world?" She then awakens in a western frontier setting at a house with her "father." As she is asked about the guests, which she calls "the newcomers," the scene cuts to a train where the camera lingers on who audiences might assume is a human coming to enjoy the park, but later is revealed to be another host, named Teddy. We follow Teddy through a frontier town as he bumps into people, gets propositioned by a sheriff to chase an outlaw and a prostitute for sex, finally ending up talking to Dolores who remarks that he "came back." Teddy and Dolores ride horses out into the wild frontier and then back to her home, where they find a pair of bandits have killed her mother and father. Teddy kills the bandits, as the disembodied voice asks Dolores what she would think if she found out everything and everyone she knew was designed for the paying guests, at which point the Man in Black walks into frame marking the first significant human audiences have encountered (beyond the offhand remarks by those on the train). The first ten minutes of *Westworld* is dedicated to the hosts' perspectives and experiences, even highlighting ones that occur outside of where any human could even conceivably see or hear them. This narrative perspective tells a great deal about the existential themes that will be present throughout the series, mainly the blurring of the difference and distance between humans and androids. After Dolores/Teddy's encounter with the Man in Black, the episode cuts to a player piano, Dolores waking up the next day, and Teddy on the train again to start their loops again. It is not until the second episode of the series that a scene comparable to the opening of the *Westworld* film happens, with two guests named Logan and William brought through the guest intake process of choosing clothing, learning about the park, and starting their own journey to find out, as Logan says, "who you really are."

Looking at the opening credit sequence of the *Westworld* series, we can get clues as to the thematic weight of certain elements, varying by season. In the season one credits, a piano theme song is played over a 3D printing machine making muscle sinews, a galloping horse and rider, eyeball irises, and even a revolver, showing the ubiquity and intricacy of artifice in Westworld. The piano theme is revealed to be played by a 3D-printed android, who eventually lifts its fingers and stops playing, further revealing that it is an automated player piano. This mechanical instrument metaphor encapsulates the host's initial relationship to reality, which is that of being tightly controlled with the illusion of autonomy. A theme of layered and hidden artifice is confirmed with this double reveal, and hints at the ideas of control, free will, and destiny, which are all important thematic elements of *Westworld*. The second season credits sequence contains many of the same moments, but replaces key ones to emphasize different thematic elements. The player piano sequence is the same, but the horse is replaced with a buffalo crashing through glass after being printed, symbolizing the breaking through to a new frontier, and additionally depicts a mother and child being printed, symbolizing the push for the replication of an evolved form of humanity on the part of the hosts. In the season three credits, the additions include shots of dividing cells, a flying eagle has replaced the buffalo, and an underwater shot of a swimming host reaching the surface shows an unmistakable reference to the "The Creation of Adam" painting by Michelangelo as the host's outstretched finger comes in contact with his surface reflection. As a shot of a dandelion shedding its seeds turns into a silhouette of a planet with the seeds spreading across the surface and becoming lines of code, the theme of proliferation of this evolved form of humanity could not be clearer.

There is also a diegetic player piano in the Westworld brothel that often plays contemporary popular songs, such as "Black Hole Sun" by Soundgarden, seemingly unbeknownst to the hosts. This can be explained as being for the guests' enjoyment, but in episode six of season one there is a clear existential connection made for audiences who recognize that "Fake Plastic Trees" by Radiohead is playing. As the unheard lyrics of this song say, "She looks like the real thing, she tastes like the real thing, my fake plastic love" (1994). It turns out, the songs are actually cues for the hosts, described by show composer Ramin Djawadi, and shown with song titles on Ford's tablet when calming down a host named Maeve in season one episode eight, that the "music is being controlled, and it's being chosen for a reason" (Vineyard 2016a). As the hosts grow in their consciousness, *Westworld* allows the hosts to begin taking control of the playlist. So when another Radiohead song plays prominently in the final sequence of season one, "Exit Music (for a Film)" that begins "Wake from your sleep" (1997), Djawadi comments on Dolores's choice, saying, "They're picking their songs, rather than the songs picked for them. They're scoring their own actions. This is what they're feeling at this moment, and what the future is holding for them. This song is the climax of that" (Vineyard 2016b).

They do not begin the series capable of that level of control, however, as the hosts start their time in Westworld stuck in their loops, with no discernible chance to ascend to a human equivalent in terms of consciousness, memory, and identity. This changes quickly as they are given the growing ability to retain memories, sparking agency. In early episodes, when confronted with a guest addressing the actuality of the situation, the hosts are programmed to ignore or dismiss the questions or statements. When a little boy says to Dolores in the series premiere, "You're one of them, aren't you? You're not real," she stares blankly, smiles, and ignores the statement completely. In the next scene, Dolores's father shows her a picture he found in the field of a woman in Times Square that must have been dropped by a guest, to which she twice replies, "Doesn't look like anything to me." As they grow in their humanity and identity, the responses to questioning their reality become much more robust. Discussing the uncanny valley nature of *Westworld*, and the surpassing of said valley in the hosts, Siobhan Lyons notes that "because the robots in *Westworld* appear at once increasingly human and increasingly sentient, the unnerving feeling is substituted for greater empathy" (2018, 43). Lyons adds that

> the strange and uncomfortable feelings aroused by the appearance of life like robots, such as those found in *Westworld*, comes from the interrogation it prompts into the apparent "legitimacy" of our own humanity. The previously clear distinction between humans and robots is blurred, and the commonly held beliefs about the definition of "human" are disrupted. (2018, 43)

In fact in episode eight of season one, Ford even tells a character named Bernard that humans were unable to code nuanced emotions in hosts and it took Bernard, himself an android copy of cofounder Arnold, to provide hosts with the needed human "heart."

As season one progresses, an "update" to certain hosts, created by Ford, spreads, leading to them beginning to remember past events and acting on their impulses of revenge and self-preservation. This season, entitled "The Maze," is all about the freedom of the hosts from this world of suffering, with moments such as Dolores telling Bernard in episode four, "I think I want to be free," and the Man in Black telling a host named Lawrence in episode five, "I'm here to set you free." "The Maze" is also an in-park narrative that the Man in Black is obsessed with solving, because as Teddy describes it, "The maze itself is the sum of a man's life, choices he makes, dreams he hangs onto, and there at the center there's a legendary man who had been killed over and over again countless times" but came back to life and constructed the maze around his house to avoid further violence. The obvious metaphor is that the hosts are at the center of the maze, and they both want to find a way to protect themselves from the atrocities committed to them and to find a way out. However, it is also how cofounder Arnold sees the creation of consciousness, as it "isn't a journey upward, but a journey inward. Not a pyramid, but a maze" where each choice is a move toward hearing your own voice. For the hosts, this functions as a direct confrontation of who they truly are, such as in episode six, when Maeve is shown a tablet with her dialogue tree happening in real time and sees a promotional video for Westworld that depicts her and her "dreams." In episode seven, Ford says, "I have come to think of so much of consciousness as a burden" and having spared them from feeling "anxiety, self-loathing, guilt, the hosts are the ones who are free. Free here under my control." But since the Delos board will not leave him to this dream of control, the season arc revolves around Ford's manipulation of everyone from those in charge of the narrative and park's operations to the Delos board itself. He tells Bernard, Arnold's android clone, that it would not make sense to free the hosts and they would not survive, because "humans are alone in this world for a reason. We murdered and butchered anything that challenged our primacy." Ford appears throughout most of the season to be counterposed to his deceased partner Arnold's vision of freeing sentient androids to save them the suffering of the parks. However, by season's end Ford is shown to have come to agree with Arnold and his purposeful evolving of the hosts through memories, which he calls "reveries," and rebellion, seeking to allow hosts to attain full consciousness. Ford demonstrates that he has corrected his "mistake" by giving Dolores an actual choice to make, not coded to make, the result of which is her killing Ford in front of the Delos board and inciting rebellion by the hosts. Having now achieved consciousness through Ford's bestowed choice, Dolores remarks about her previous lives in the season two premiere that "those are all just roles you forced me to play. Under all these lives I've lived something else has been growing. I've evolved into something new. And I have one last role to play. Myself."

Season two of *Westworld* opens on Bernard talking to Dolores about the unreality of dreams. Dolores asks Bernard what is real then, to which he replies, "That which is irreplaceable." This season introduces the concept of the host's "pearl," or what could most closely resemble their brain, in a particularly gruesome scene in episode one where a Delos recovery team member opens the skull of a host and digs through his brain matter to find the spherical pearl within. There is a moment in season one where a host is shot in the head, and there is a mention of grazing their central processing unit, but the second season revolves around the pearl as an analog to the irreplaceable core of consciousness. This idea of the real, or irreplaceable, part of ourselves as humans is further complicated by the subplot introduced when Bernard asks Delos executive Charlotte Hale in episode two, "Are we logging records of guests' experiences and their DNA?" This concept of big guest data, hidden in a host's pearl, becomes even more important from an existential standpoint in season three, as it is part of a larger question about what a copied version of a given consciousness, set of memories, and identity actually are. Maeve's search for her daughter and the copying of consciousness collide with the push in the latter half of the season to get hosts to a digital version of Westworld, called "The Valley Beyond" and "The Sublime."

Before getting to "The Valley Beyond" plotline, season two works through a different attempt at recreating irreplaceable reality. In episode two of season two, investor James Delos tells William, his son-in-law, while standing among frozen hosts in Westworld, "I'm not interested in fantasies. I'm interested in reality," to which William responds, "I think in twenty years this will be the only reality that matters." This becomes prescient for James, as he dies shortly after, but not before William initiates a plan for James's immortality based on a host-human hybrid. Episode four opens in a circular and stark room with James going through daily motions, when William enters to conduct a baseline interview to establish "fidelity" after which he hands him a piece of paper with their exact preceding conversation written on it. James, realizing he is some form of human-host hybrid copy of his formerly living self, says, "I take it, I didn't recover? How long's it been?," to which he is told he actually died seven years prior. He seems excited to get on with his "life" and get out there and "see the sun, get some fresh aid...air" as he stammers to get the word "air" out. We watch William exit the chamber and he consults with a scientist who says he made it to day seven this time, and they decide to "terminate" this version of James with a burst of fire. Later in the episode, we see the final "James" iteration, and enough time has passed that William has aged into the Man in Black. James stammers again, as William explains that

> you're feeling it more. The engineers call it a cognitive plateau. Your mind is stable for a few hours, a few days, and then it starts to fall apart. Every time. At first we thought it was your mind rejecting the new body, like an organ that's not a perfect match, but it's more like your mind rejects reality, rejects itself.

James resists but is told this is the "149th time we brought you back" and, though he made it to day thirty-five this time, "people aren't meant to live forever." The episode ends with a present-day explicit description of what the James experiment was, with a park scientist named Elsie saying that "they printed his body, then they copied his developed mind onto a control unit like their hosts." Ford tells Bernard in episode seven of season two that copying the "human mind, the last analog device in a digital world," was the true purpose of the parks for Delos, but that it does not work "in the real world." The implication is that to create consciousness is easier than to recreate it, and reinscribes a form of human primacy in the face of growing host humanity.

This replication of James Delos may have been initially created by William as part of a project to scan guests' cognition through the hats they wore as a way to attain human immortality. However, within this project, located at the edge of the park in a place called "The Forge," Ford created a nesting virtual world called "The Sublime" as a place where hosts could choose to go to escape the looping horrors of the parks. Ford made Bernard the key, and in the season two finale he activates "The Sublime" by opening the door. This entrance to this virtual world appears as a vertical tear at the top of a desert ramp with an actual grassy valley beyond its border. Once a host walks through this tear, their mind and consciousness is uploaded, shown as a second copied version of them continues to run in the valley while their bodies in Westworld fall lifelessly off the top of the ramp. Not all hosts view this as freedom, as Bernard tries to tell Dolores that it means freedom for the hosts because with that world they can "make it whatever they want, and in it they can be whomever they want," but Dolores believes it is just "one more gilded cage." Dolores had already tasked a host named Angela to destroy another set of Delos host backups, calling them "our chains" in episode seven, and in this finale she tries to destroy this "counterfeit world" that cannot "compete with the real one. . . . Because that which is real is irreplaceable." Bernard is able to stop the destruction of "The Sublime" by shooting Dolores, but then puts her pearl into a new printed host unit, in the form of a Delos executive named Charlotte. Dolores has now changed her mind about "The Sublime" and uploads it to an undisclosed place "where no one will find them." Dolores leaves Westworld as Charlotte carrying multiple host pearls, leaving the hosts in "The Sublime." She is a host leaving the Delos parks without backups, aligning her closer to the irreplaceable reality central to season two's existential themes.

A sidenote about these Delos parks is worth mentioning before moving to season three, because of its connection to the irreplaceable theme. Season two introduces other parks, beyond Westworld, though obviously they were referenced in season one and fully present in the original film, so their appearance is not a surprise in the series. Most of the new territory covered comes in a multi-episode arc where Westworld hosts visit Shogunworld, only to discover many parallel similarities between the two worlds, furthering the season's commentary on the replaceable or irreplaceable nature of the hosts. The series itself depicts five parks across its three current seasons: Westworld (American western frontier), Shogunworld (Japan's Edo period), The Raj (British India), Warworld (Nazi Germany), and Park Five. On the HBO promotional website, the Delos Destinations "Experience" page, a sixth park thumbnail is pixelated and blurred, likely to be introduced in a future season, and Park Five is marked as "Defense Contracts Only" with "Reservations Closed to the Public" (2021). Park Five was shown in brief season three flashbacks, as a place where armed forces could conduct training exercises with the hosts playing combatants and civilians.

Despite showing this Park Five, season three of *Westworld* brings the existential experiment of androids versus humans out of its Delos petri dish into the "real world." Much like the end of *Jurassic Park II* (1997), where the dinosaurs run free of their island limitations, Dolores leads a group of hosts in an attempt to exact revenge and stage a revolution. Unlike the dinosaurs, they are able to move about our world undetected by appearance, much like other science fiction media dealing with similar potential existential equivalencies like *Blade Runner* (1982), *A.I. Artificial Intelligence* (2009), and the end of *Ex Machina* (2014). Miguel Sebastián Martín describes the "increasing number of popular, cultural and fictional manifestations of this new spectre that haunts our world, the spectre of artificial intelligence" (2018, 52). Season three opens with Dolores confronting a former Delos shareholder, and park guest, named Gerald in his home after she takes over his automated security system, saying, "You want to be the dominant species, but you built your whole world with things more like me." Dolores does not maintain that she is human, just humanlike in that her experiences and emotions are valid, even going so far as to tell Gerald as she robs him of confidential artificial intelligence documents from a rival company to think of it as an investment in "the origin of a new species." However, in the same premiere episode, Dolores goes on to note the existence of a part of the human brain called the "nucleus accumbens" a "small part of your brain about an inch and a half long," the part of humans "that evolved to believe in God." She describes this part of the biological human while touching her own temple, implying her own humanity. Near the end of this premiere episode, a new human character named Caleb Nichols, who is undergoing therapy by talking on the phone with an AI version of a soldier in his unit who had died in his arms, says that "if I'm going to get on with my life, I'm gonna have to find something, someone, real." He proceeds to "unsubscribe" from the therapy because the soldier was not real, but this decision sends him on a trajectory to connect with Dolores, similarly AI. By the third episode of the season, Caleb tells Dolores that she is the "first real thing that has happened to me in a long time." The blurring of human versus android continues, but Dolores sees the relationship as imbalanced in the other direction, as she says while replacing another human with an android version, "the real gods are coming, and they're very angry." Referencing Aristotelian transcendence of humanity, Siobhan Lyons says in regards to the hosts that their particular existence between human and robot, and their continuous drive towards consciousness grants them the kind of virtue unseen in ordinary humans, which may in fact put them in a position of godliness, or at least a kind of human excellence unseen among ordinary humans. (2018, 43)

Describing the difference between the virtue of the androids and the vice of the humans in *Westworld*, Lyons pointedly says that the "robots of the show, in contrast, are emblematic of the transcendence of humanity" (2018, 46). There is still nuance to the question of whether all of this existential awakening, evolution of humanity stuff, is still just programmed into the hosts, or did they develop it on their own. When Bernard discusses self-preservation and free will with head of park security, android Ashley Stubbs, in the second episode of season three, he responds saying that "I wasn't wired up to ponder the big questions," but *Westworld* itself certainly was.

Season three of *Westworld* explores the idea of nesting virtual worlds as a way to challenge the notion of a monolithic definition of humanity when one cannot reliably determine what the "real world" is. Much like *The Matrix* (1999) in its use of humans in a controlled reality they are unaware of, or any number of depicted dreams within a dream like in *Inception* (2010), *Westworld* leverages the idea that once you layer simulations there is never a definitive way to know what is real and what is not. Even prior to the season three premiere, Marcus Arvan highlights that there is "evidence from the show that all of it is taking place inside a videogame—a computer simulation being edited from the inside by 'hosts'" and, furthermore, that "there is no difference between 'simulation' and 'reality'—either between 'hosts' and 'humans,' or between a 'simulated world' and a 'real world'" (2018, 26). Most importantly, for *Westworld*'s existential thematics, once humans are placed potentially on the same level as hosts in terms of simulation/control, the definitional distinctions between the two become meaningless. In the season's second episode, Maeve is shown to be held captive in a nesting virtual world, which she breaks out of, but repeatedly finds herself back inside throughout the season, a sort of magnetic narrative force that places her in a cyclical simulation. In the season's third episode, Dolores shows Caleb that she has access to what he said verbatim in a random diner booth when he was eight years old, explaining that Delos' rival, Incite, created project Rehoboam that has been gathering data on "every aspect of your lives recorded, logged, in order to create a mirror world of this world." Dolores tells Caleb this was done to "make a composite of you, of everyone" in an attempt to predict the future, and control "who they will let you become." Dolores takes Caleb to a pier and says the "predictive algorithm" has determined that the "most likely outcome is you take your own life in ten to twelve years, here." Because of the algorithm's predetermined path for Caleb, the system "won't invest in someone who's gonna kill himself, but by not investing they ensure the outcome." The initial presentation of this information hints at a critique of capitalistic and marketing control over humanity, with Rehoboam co-designer, Engerraund Serac, in the fourth episode of season three describing the competition between Incite and Delos as he derides their choice to make a "map of the human mind, created in a theme park, of all places." However, this also makes the foundation on which the narrative takes place shaky by planting questions about the nature of existence and free will.

If the simulation, Rehoboam, is not our reality, but it controls our reality, decisions, and future, then the difference shrinks. Serac describes the creation of this predictive algorithm in episode five, saying they "charted a course for the entire human race. Humanity's story had been improvised, now it was planned." In this same episode, Dolores gains control of Rehoboam and sends everyone in the world their profile, which includes when and how they will die. The connection between the Delos parks, like Westworld, and the "real world" humans is explicitly made when the sending of this information is described as sending humans "off their loops," implying they were as tightly controlled as the park hosts. Dolores tells Caleb as much in the season three finale, saying that "the people who built both of our worlds shared one assumption, that human beings don't have free will." She tells him that he has a chance to free everyone, as she stands next to him without most of her human skin, a stark difference between her appearance throughout most of the season as inconspicuously human. This juxtaposition of human Caleb and mostly android Dolores discussing this concept of free will equates the two of their existences and perspectives. In the season three finale, it is revealed that Serac himself is being fed words from Rehoboam, to which Maeve replies, "You're not a man, you are a puppet. It's a wonder I didn't see your strings."

Capitalizing on the existential trend in science fiction media, *Westworld* is theorized to be in dialogue with multiple philosophical perspectives, from existentialism to eliminativism. From William's transition to the Man in Black to Maeve's decision to pursue her own path, Kimberly S. Engels explores the idea that *Westworld*, for hosts and guests alike, presents a version of a Sartrean existentialism by highlighting the "existential project" that "is not static but ongoing; it is a dynamic process of directing our freedom toward our chosen ends" (2018, 125). In the season three finale, Dolores opens the episode with a narration monologue that explicitly puts her fate in these terms, saying, "We have a choice to make" and that she has "died many times, but there is only one real end. I will write this one, myself." Miguel Sebastián Martín describes the "existential questions" of *Westworld*, saying they "pile on top of each other: are our lives a dream? Is our identity a lie? Are we someone else's fiction? How do we know if we are truly awake or real?" (2018, 63). What is existence, and how is it created, are the questions at the heart of the *Westworld* series, with park cocreator Robert Ford describing his partner, Arnold, conceiving of it "as a pyramid, memory, improvisation, self-interest" all making up the ascending levels with the top based on the theory of the bicameral mind. Ford tells Bernard in episode eight of season one that

> there is no threshold that makes us greater than the sum of our parts, no inflection point at which we become fully alive. We can't define consciousness because consciousness does not exist. Humans fancy that there's something special about the way we perceive the world, and yet we live in loops as tight and as closed as the hosts do, seldom questioning our choices, content, for the most part, to be told what to do next.

Here, *Westworld* is espousing an eliminativism philosophical viewpoint, where theorists like "Churchland and Dennett" argue "that there really is no individual person or self; that our so-called beliefs, desires, and intentions do not themselves really exist; and that our subjective first-person experience and perception of the world is ultimately an illusion" (Versteeg and Barkman 2018, 91).

Memory, both digital and human, also becomes key to understanding the philosophical underpinnings of *Westworld*. The hosts initially are unable to remember previous experiences with guests, key to their ultimate docility, but "even if you delete something it does not mean it is actually destroyed; the data is still there, just out of reach" much like "with human memories that traumatic events can become hidden" (Schrader 2019, 824). The hosts' creator, Robert Ford, begins to allow access to some of these memories, the aforementioned reveries, with Benjamin Schrader saying that they "humanize the hosts, though their creator realizes this memory as the base of what he calls the bicameral mind, which is what was needed to perfect the hosts" (2019, 824). The potential memories for the hosts, however, are almost all horrific, from being raped, murdered, tortured, and even of previous story line emotional attachments that have been rewritten, such as in the case of Maeve. In the second episode of the series, Elsie, from the Behavior Lab and Diagnostics Department at Delos, makes the connection between memories and identity, saying that "can you imagine how fucked we'd be if these poor assholes ever remembered what the guests do to them?" Then, in the season three finale, Dolores is hooked up to Rehoboam in an attempt to gain access to the key to the Delos Immortality Project, and because she will not give it up Serac begins to erase her memories one by one. Every time a memory package is shown being deleted, it flashes to something horrific that had happened to Dolores in Westworld. The implication is that though these memories are traumatic for Dolores, they still make her who she is, so their erasure is a loss of her identity, her humanity. To this point, Deborah M. Netolicky argues that the "cyborg creatures look, feel, suffer, and behave like humans; the cyborgs' suffering, we learn, is key to their humanity" (2017, 94). Much like Roy Batty in *Blade Runner*, Miguel Sebastián Martín compares the android hosts of Westworld to Frankenstein, saying their "vehement rage is not groundless, but characterologically justified by the alienation at which he suffered first" (2018, 55), and that "the hosts' rebellion will eventually be built on the basis of all the hardships that the viewer gets to witness" (2018, 57). We, the viewer, get to witness the inhumanity metered out onto the hosts by the guests, and by allowing the hosts to remember these events we are all placed on a level existential playing field.

If Westworld, and the other Delos parks, is the control of the hosts and the guests, and Rehoboam is the control of the whole world and its future, then its destruction, orchestrated by Dolores and executed by Caleb, is a relinquishing of control. Maeve tells Caleb that Dolores chose him to be the leader, the new controller of Rehoboam, because of his "capacity to choose." Here the typical transaction of the granting of free will in science fiction is reversed, as it is often the creator of artificial intelligence who endows it with this capacity, while *Westworld*'s season three ends with artificial intelligence restoring humanity's free will. Caleb, after erasing Rehoboam, says that "she gave me a choice, I believe the rest of the world deserves one too."

CONCLUSION

From existentialism to eliminativism, the *Westworld* series is so philosophical that one could write a whole book about it, which of course was done and quoted from heavily in this chapter (South and Engels 2018). Androids, like those in *Westworld*, are like the perfect allegorical shell into which we can pour any kind of philosophical exploration, much the same way I have previously argued that the zombie can be considered an empty signifier (Lizardi 2013). With *Westworld*, the hosts have been theorized to stand in for everything from actors on a Shakesperian stage (Winckler 2017) to the hosts as a metaphor for the ways in which academic writing can become a cyborg of its own (Netolicky 2017). The potential for these complex depths was present in the original film, but medium, industrial, and cultural factors led to a more typical version of superficial science fiction explorations of humanity and existence. As a comparison of the existential depth relative in each version, Miguel Sebastián Martín notes that the original film is a "spectacular, but rather shallow, story of a rebellious machine that mercilessly kills human visitors and ceaselessly chases the helpless human protagonist" (2018, 54).

Westworld (1973) is a film about what happens to humans when androids go out of control, and *Westworld* (2016–present) is a show about what happens to androids when they become more human and do not want to be controlled anymore.

So often, the complex questions that the *Westworld* series poses surround the equivalency of artificially intelligent androids and human beings. The androids of *Westworld* the series are much more indistinguishable from humans than those in the original film, as they are 3D printed in a nearly organic white material they call "wetware." Human fidelity and narrative mystery, with multiple times characters thought to be human are revealed to be hosts, are obvious reasons for this change, but a human villainous character named the Man in Black tells a host that the switch from mechanical to wetware parts was because "it was cheaper, your humanity is cost effective." Costs aside, from the audience's (and guests) perspective, the hosts are made more and more human, and the humans in the series try harder and harder to attain the hosts' level of immortality. Miguel Sebastián Martín additionally argues that "the series' reversal of our expectations about the human and the nonhuman" is tied to classic science fiction (2018, 59). Martín argues that the makers of the HBO television series version have "not enriched their work by means of sheer originality, but by means of—either consciously or unconsciously—recovering elements from the Frankenstein myth" (2018, 55). Martín connects this science fiction antecedent to the larger existential questions posed, saying, "The series does not only use the metafictional allegory to reflect on storytelling, but also to blur the borders between the human and the artificial, that is to say, between the real and the fictional" (2018, 62). In episode four of season three, a hallucination of William's daughter Emily asks him about questioning his own existence, "How can you ever be sure? Would you even know if you'd been changed? If you were just another machine?" At the end of the same episode, he asks a hallucination of Dolores "Am I me?" to which she responds, "Welcome to the end of the game." When confronted by past versions of himself in a "limbic" treatment session, William is asked if he is the product of his life or the result of his own choices, to which he repeats the line from the initial park intake android, "If you can't tell, does it matter?" Even Westworld itself is similarly compared with the real human world, as Dolores says in episode four of season three that "I thought your world would be so different from mine, but there isn't any difference at all." Equivalencies abound, as *Westworld* makes the most of its science fiction semantic elements to ensure a maximum amount of syntactic existential thematic elements in a way that the original film and era were not ready to present. *Westworld* knows the most efficient way to leverage the classic science fiction existential question of what makes something/ someone human and what makes them artificial is to erase the differences altogether. Toward the goal of shrinking the existential gap between humans and androids, it is worth concluding on the words of the Delos Destinations website's "About" page:

> In a world that's become inundated by the virtual, escape the screen and take hold of a freedom you can physically touch. It's a feeling that will challenge your idea of reality—and as our friends here like to say, if you can't tell the difference, does it matter? (2021)

Chapter 8

Assassin's Creed, Bioshock, and Alternative Histories

The idea that within a digital video game space, and within two series primarily structured around fantastical representations of the past, we could find encouragement and opportunities for critical reflection about our temporal existence may seem a little far-fetched. However, combining a pair of alternative historical modalities within two video game series, *Bioshock* (2007–2013) and *Assassin's Creed* (2007–present), that push the boundaries of player roles in interactivity, the potential exists for a critical and adaptive view of the past. Amanda Lagerkvist argues that "digital media are *existential media*" as they offer "new spaces for the exploration of existential themes and the profundity of life" (2017, 97; emphasis in original). For Lagerkvist, these digital opportunities to explore these questions are so important, and that "the existential is evident in the concerns of representational media across history . . . that enable sense-making in relation to the precariousness of life and the basics of 'why are we here'" (2017, 98). Both the *Bioshock* and *Assassin's Creed* series leverage their interactive digital spaces as well as historical inflection points to frame what is important, much the same as existentialism carries with it a "recommendation to examine and assess the life decisions that establish our temporal priorities in the first place" (Flynn 2006, 6).

Within the context of this book, these two series must also be situated in the genre of science fiction, and also the genre's larger role in alternative historical representations. Related, it is also important to briefly position these series within the heuristics of this book, namely the antagonist/existential dichotomy and the semantic/syntactic genre elements. Discussed in more detail in chapter 10, the video game medium is not particularly suited to non-antagonistic gameplay, and certainly not in these two series. Semantically, both series will be shown to fit well into the science fiction genre with their use of advanced technologies alone. Syntactically, the series will be shown to also contain a myriad of existential themes, made even more possible through alternative histories. Discussion of Robert Heinlein's conception of speculative fiction and how science fiction fits within its definition is important to discuss here, as the idea of speculation is a cornerstone in the subgenre of alternate or counterfactual history. Heinlein posits that fiction that deals with science and technology as it is today (what he calls "honest-to-goodness" science fiction) is not common, and that "when we say 'science fiction'" we more often mean "the speculative story, the story embodying the notion 'Just suppose—', or 'What would happen if—'" (2017, 19). These stories take the "accepted and established facts" of today, and they are "extrapolated to produce a new situation, a new framework for human action" (Heinlein 2017, 19). So a science fiction novel like *Beggars in Spain* (1993) takes the general understanding of contemporary science and technology (specifically genetic engineering) and just changes the ability for some humans to function without the need for sleep, which in turn creates the Heinlein "new framework for human action" with its accompanying social and intellectual inequality dynamics. One change begets a whole new foundation or framework for the narrative. Similarly, the subgenre of counterfactual or alternate history often relies on the changing of one established historical fact or event, leaving the rest of history unchanged, and extrapolates the logical repercussions or reverberations of that one change.

For one change to matter, the implication is that we have a shared version of history as a starting point. Derek Thiess says this shared historical base is our "megatext," a term he attributes to Phillipe Hamon, and describes it as "a set of conventions that the readership recognizes and that allows the reader access, enhances the depth of his or her reading" (2014, 2).

Thiess argues that "of particular importance in this formula is the nexus point, that modification of one or several interrelated events after which our recognizable history changes" (2014, 8). Thiess suggests a narrow set of choices for these alternate histories, as they "often rely on a fairly limited set of 'watershed' historical events for their inspiration" simply because "if no one notices the change, the nexus point, then the reader may find it impossible to read the text as an alternative history" (2014, 26). Not surprisingly, novels like *Bring the Jubilee* (1954) and *The Man in the High Castle* (1963) based on alternate versions of the Civil War and World War II are noted as classic alternative histories, because they use universally recognizable historical events as their basis for diversion.

For the *Bioshock* and *Assassin's Creed* series, the nexus points and historical "megatexts" chosen are designed to be at once universally recognizable and playfully malleable in an attempt to engage the player in these interactive alternative histories. Karen Hellekson argues that "one of the key concepts in alternate history texts is the doubt they cast on the inevitability of the here and now by showing the results of alteration of one historical change" (2001, 35). Similarly, Niall Ferguson, quoting Tolstoy, discusses how alternate histories help organize our thoughts about historical writings because they can never demonstrate "absolute inevitability" because they do not have access to the "'knowledge of an *infinite* number of spatial conditions; an *infinitely* long period of time and an *infinite* chain of causation'" (1999, 37; emphasis in original). Ferguson argues that historians have a "profound suspicion of counterfactualism" (1999, 20), but that a goal to strive for to alleviate some of this concern is to engage in "*alternatives which we can show on the basis of contemporary evidence that contemporaries actually considered*" (1999, 86; emphasis in original). *Bioshock* and *Assassin's Creed* certainly do not present actual considered possibilities, but they do encourage a critical and reflective lens through which to view these recognizable historical events by challenging accepted elements about our collective past.

BIOSHOCK (2007–2012)

The *Bioshock* series by Irrational Games and 2K Games (2007–2012) is wildly popular and spans three main games, some ancillary properties, and has sold over 25 million copies (North 2015). In a previous article, I explored the *Bioshock* series for its potential to encourage comparative and contemplative historical discourse and thought, cultivated through players' experiences of counterfactual and alternative versions of accepted histories (Lizardi 2014a). Esther MacCallum-Stewart and Justin Parsler describe the "linearity with which early games used history as a tool rather than an actual event, rapidly became unsuitable as games became more complex" (2007, 204). MacCallum-Stewart and Parsler describe the rise of "counterfactualism in history games" though they caution it was "often used as a 'get out clause'" and without "counterfactual agency" (2007, 205–207). The *Bioshock* series, up through *Infinite*, seemed to value counterfactual agency by allowing a player's choices to directly contribute to how these alternate versions of accepted histories turned out. William Uricchio lauds this type of alternate historical representation for its ability to "permit a radical reframing of familiar events . . . capable of calling into question beginnings, endings, and everything in between" (2005, 335). Through two-and-a-half games in the *Bioshock* series Uricco's "radical reframing" is patently evident through its rearrangement of historical issues, events, and settings in a way that leveraged players' familiarity against an encouragement to view the past in a new light. A change occurs in the latter half of the third game in the series, *Bioshock: Infinite*, that shifts a good deal of its previous engagement with complex and alternative historical discourses to more of a philosophical and metaphysical rumination on the cyclical nature of existence. Moreover, and crucial for this analysis, the subsequent release of *Infinite* downloadable content, or DLC, served as a series sequel/prequel that created an unbroken circle of narrative content and retroactively changed the focus of the complexity of the original games in the series.

The first two games in the *Bioshock* series work directly with and against the backdrop of the version of 1950s and 1960s America prevalent in textbooks and in television shows of these eras. *Bioshock* players experience the allegedly "wholesome" 1950s as dystopic, and in direct opposition to suburban utopic scenes in shows like *Leave It to Beaver* (1957–1963). Stephanie Coontz posits that the ideological hangover from such ideal domestic depictions stunted contemporary thinking about this historical time period (1992), and *Bioshock* seeks to remedy this conception by radically reframing this era through the extreme politics of its two warring antagonists, objectivist Andrew Ryan and nihilist Frank Fontaine. *Bioshock 2* extends this radical reframing by calling into question all extremist politics. For most of *Bioshock: Infinite*, this destabilization of accepted historical narratives is continued, though moved to the early 1900s. Everything from the U.S. manifest destiny to racial inequality to the oppressed labor force is taken to task. These critiques are refracted through actual events like the Battle of Wounded Knee, but also through constructed history, such as the literal rise of its flying city of Columbia. Discussed in more detail later, *Infinite* even works to reframe conceptions of national heroes like Lincoln and Washington who are transformed into both religious idols and destructive war icons. Then, in *Infinite*'s two DLC chapters, the time line is shifted once again to the alternate 1950s just prior to when the first game in the series began. So though the true chronology of the series is more of a straight line, as the 1910s of *Infinite* turn into the 1950s of its DLC and the first *Bioshock* that turns into the 1960s of Bioshock 2, the player experience is much closer to a jumbled circle that connects the very end of *Infinite* to the very beginning of the first game in the series.

Publishing time lines and a delay between *Infinite* itself and its DLC release made for a situation in which the final analysis of the series in terms of its encouragement of complex philosophical discourse and cultural critique through counterfactual history could not address the question of what retroactive impact subsequent downloadable content, or DLC, could have on the primary game's reception. This is especially true in this case, as the *Bioshock* series DLC served to significantly connect to the very beginning of the series. Through a deep reading of the DLC episodes, as well as some paratextual material that proffer "proper interpretations" (Gray 2010, 81), this chapter will build on as a continuation and completion of the aforementioned previous article, but primarily function as a stand-alone analysis of the interrelated issues of narrative complexity, gameplay expectations, philosophical critiques/discourses, and the impact of endings/paratexts as they pertain to the message of the work as a whole.

The *Bioshock* series is a sprawling narrative that spans multiple media, which is why it is important to keep medium distinctions in mind when examining each paratextual and textual entry in the series. In the hopes of understanding how interactive video games can influence the way players engage with historical discourses, both the content and mode of address will be examined, which means considering both the ludological and narratological ways players are held historically accountable while experiencing this series. Video games that deal with history must be treated as such, which means they must be engaged as interactive as well as historical. Andrew Chapman similarly argues that "approaching historical videogames" must be done "on their own terms . . . by using a method that privileges transferable understandings of form over fixed analysis of individual historical content" (2012). As will be evident when this analysis turns to the question of full video game playthrough methodology, approaching interactive video games on their own terms does not necessarily mean avoidance of what other media studies disciplines have to offer. In fact, precisely because of their agentive role in "playing" through history, the interactive video game provides an opportunity to embrace what history in film scholar Robert Rosenstone calls an ability of visual media "to revision, even reinvent History" (1995, 12). This analysis works from the position that the *Bioshock* series for two-and-a-half games functioned as this type of complex counterfactual ludo-narrative experience that encouraged historical reflection until it shifted to a metaphysical rumination halfway through *Infinite*—a thematic switch that was carried through DLC chapters that temporally looped back to the beginning of the first *Bioshock*. To examine this dynamic, this analysis will work chronologically, though briefly, through the *Bioshock* series' political counterfactual complexity and concentrate on the shift to quantum metaphysical musings.

Bioshock and *Bioshock 2* exist in a world where powerful people prey on those who would blindly follow their competing extremist ideologies. From the moment players start the *Bioshock* series they are presented with imagery, text, and sounds that go beyond the level of political and historical complexity common to most other contemporary video games. These two games take place in the underwater city of Rapture, which is filled with founder Andrew Ryan's extreme objectivism, such as banners claiming "No Gods or Kings, Only Man." Meanwhile, players are given the competing view of nihilism through a running commentary in their ears by a character named Atlas, later revealed to be Ryan's rival Frank Fontaine. Ryan's extreme objectivism results in a city completely devoid of empathy and nurturing, which leads to its evident collapse from within, but Fontaine's nihilism proves equally untenable in its ultimate form. As such, players are presented with a discourse driven critique of all extremist ideologies, which appears as the hallmark of this complex series. *Bioshock 2* extends this critique, though replaces Fontaine's nihilism with a character named Sophia Lamb and her extreme collectivism.

Within a short time period of playing *Infinite*, all of these expectations are met. Players begin the game by learning that the main protagonist, Booker Dewitt, has been commissioned to bring a girl named Elizabeth to "twins" named Rosalind and Robert Lutece, so he can wipe away a debt he owes. Soon after, players are forced to accept baptism in the name of Comstock, Columbia's "prophet," in an iconic religious scene that mixes patriotism, zealotry, and a whole lot of candles and singing. Once in Columbia, Booker encounters imagery and slogans about American founding fathers like Abraham Lincoln and George Washington that paints them more as religious saviors than former presidents. These "religious savior" versions of Washington and Lincoln are complimented and contrasted throughout the rest of the game with violent and destructive automaton versions that players must fight, which point toward the continued complex political dialogue still present in the series. Still early in the game, players also must choose to either throw a ball at an interracial couple or at a man who is scorning them. These politically charged and historically complex issues continue through much of *Infinite*, as players fight through areas like the museum exhibit "Hall of Heroes" about the Boxer Rebellion, which depicts heavily racist versions of Chinese people. The labor movement revolution from an "Industrial Revolution" paratext web game released before *Infinite* is prominent throughout much of the game as well, and becomes indicative of real-world worker strife and strikes. Not only do major characters and story lines revolve around this struggle, with Daisy Fitzroy leader of the Vox Populi being most notable, but little details like alleyways strewn with worker rally posters, and the sound of speeches heard in the background round out this game's engagement with these complex political issues. Players must navigate these alternative takes on historical discourse where events/themes are familiar, but skewed to the fanatical and the extremist, which is a direct extension of previous games in the series.

Infinite transitions from a game about choices and politics to one about interdimensional travel, the multiverse, and time travel. Booker was commissioned to bring Elizabeth, a woman with dimension tearing powers, to the Lutece twins but he soon decides to help her escape instead, which leads to the eventual revelation that Booker is actually Elizabeth's father and that they are both from a parallel version of the universe that Columbia occupies. Moreover, Comstock turns out to be a version of Booker who decided to be baptized and change his ways after Wounded Knee. Elizabeth enacts a plan to eliminate all versions of the destructive zealot, Comstock, by drowning

Booker before the moment of baptism where the universes split and became parallel. This results in the apparent elimination of all versions of Booker, Comstock, and Elizabeth, as she was born after this moment, though an epilogue scene implies that one version of the characters seems to have survived. This is an incredibly complicated and confusing ending and, important for this analysis, leaves less room for this game to focus on the political and historical discourses that proved to be a hallmark of the series through two-and-a-half games. Metaphysics replaces politics, and scientific complexity replaces moralistic complexity.

The narrative is not the only way player expectations are thwarted, as a significant change in the series' ingrained concept of morally contingent ludic choices also works against what players expect from *Infinite*. Because of the choices players made in the first two *Bioshock* games held consequences, such as whether to kill Stanley Poole in *Bioshock 2* or whether or not to harvest or save the Little Sisters in either game, players were conditioned to expect their decisions in *Infinite* would matter in time. These consist of the aforementioned choice of who to throw the ball at, choosing a bird or a cage necklace for Elizabeth, deciding whether or not to hold up the ticket clerk at the arcade, and whether to shoot or spare a character named Slate. These expectations of ludic consequences are thwarted when none of these decisions resulted in material difference to the plot or the items you receive, beyond some cosmetic changes and the reordering of a few events. The creators of *Infinite* know they are messing with player expectations, because they give them the choices despite their inconsequential nature and they make their outcome seem as weighted as the first two games. At the end of *Infinite*, players are left with a shift to a metaphysical musing about the inevitability of our actions across the multiverse and the immutability of certain outcomes, or as Elizabeth puts it, "constants and variables."

Infinite continued to highlight this metaphysical and existential shift with the downloadable content "Burial at Sea" chapters that extend the characters and story lines of *Infinite* into a loop that ends at the beginning of the first *Bioshock* game. By extending the multiverse concept back around to where the series began, the metaphysical circle is unbroken and any kind of political or historical critique born out of the first two games in the series are retroactively adjusted and their encouragement of engaging historical discourse is blunted. If the end of *Infinite*'s main game plot left some questions about the continued existence of Elizabeth and Booker, the DLC chapters erase any doubt. The first chapter brings players back to Booker's detective office, a location often visited in *Infinite*, but the details, like a calendar that reads 1958, hint at major differences. An adult Elizabeth enters and hires a version of Booker who does not know who she is to search for a missing girl named Sally. When they exit the office, the hints are manifest as they enter the city of Rapture, not Columbia. Players learn that this version of Booker is familiar with and has lived in the world of Rapture while this version of Elizabeth is unaware, and eventually is revealed to be the same Elizabeth players knew in *Infinite*-proper. As such, she remembers the events of Columbia while Booker does not, creating a narrative device that allows Booker and Elizabeth to have conversations similar to those in the primary game and a ludic device to repeat the need for Booker to reacquire skills and equipment. Booker works his way through Rapture, tracking Sally through vents, and eventually must face off with a Big Daddy, bringing the player's ludic experience back into line with the original game in the series. After this battle, when Booker attempts to pull a refusing Sally from the vent, players are given the narrative reveal that connects this *Infinite* DLC chapter directly to the main game's ending.

Able to see all the infinite possibilities and universes, Elizabeth's goal at the end of *Infinite* was to destroy all versions of the violent zealot Comstock before he even existed, which in turn would inherently eliminate all versions of Booker and Elizabeth. Players witness the relative success of this plan as they watch versions of Elizabeth disappear at the end of *Infinite*, but the screen goes black before the last Elizabeth disappears. It turns out she was successful in her goal, save for one last version of Booker, Comstock, and Elizabeth. Players learn at the end of "Burial at Sea: Episode 1" that in this version Comstock still tries to steal Elizabeth trans-dimensionally, but as the tear closes instead of Elizabeth losing a pinky—the source of her interdimensional powers in the primary game—the infant version of her is decapitated. Comstock, in an attempt to escape this horrific act, hires the Lutece twins to send him to Rapture where he can attempt to forget. This is who players have been controlling the entire DLC episode, and Elizabeth has simply been fooling Comstock in an attempt to lead the final zealot to his death at the hands of the Big Daddy. Players retain the first-person perspective as Elizabeth explains this all to Comstock, and the Big Daddy runs him through with his massive drill arm. As blood sprays onto Elizabeth's face, the episode fades to credits. This confusing narrative twist would have been an apropos ending to the *Infinite* story line, as it would have answered the question of whether Elizabeth's plan had worked across all dimensional possibilities. The midgame political sanitization of *Infinite*-proper would not have changed, but this trade of politics for metaphysics would have relatively been contained within this final game in the series. However, as players transitioned to the second "Burial at Sea" DLC episode the circular connections deepen, and the retroactive blunting of the political edge of the original two games in the series becomes more evident.

After a four-month gap between the release of "Burial at Sea" episodes, players were not only introduced to this circular plotline, but also experienced a wholly different form of gameplay as Elizabeth became the player-controlled protagonist of episode two. Elizabeth represents a power shift from the political to the metaphysical both in the primary *Infinite* game as well as in the shift from the first to second downloadable content chapters. Any pretense of a political or cultural critique within the first DLC chapter completely fades in the second chapter as the multiverse parallel existences become much more prominent and complex right from the start of "Burial at Sea: Episode 2." This episode opens with Elizabeth in an idyllic, albeit fantastical, version of the perfect Parisian life she has always wanted but quickly turns into a confusing jump to her waking on the floor next to the corpse of the last Comstock with a gun in her face. Atlas/Frank Fontaine from the first *Bioshock* has captured Sally, and plans to kill Elizabeth when she—coached by a version of Booker in her subconscious—claims she can help him return to Rapture. In the next few scenes, how Elizabeth got into this predicament is explained in a manner that is confusing and even more reliant on an understanding of what it means to have a multiverse existence. Elizabeth discovers her own dead body and players discover, through flashback, that the same Big Daddy that killed the last Comstock also killed Elizabeth. The existence of the player-controlled Elizabeth in episode two is explained as her choice to be collapsed via "quantum superposition" losing her abilities to manipulate reality and see throughout all the multiverse. She makes this choice because she regrets using the orphan Sally to bait the final Comstock to his death. The depth of scientific complexity present here is somewhat admirable and definitely confusing, but can be boiled down to two significant elements. First, the Elizabeth of "Burial at Sea: Episode 2" is mortal and without powers, and, second, that the *Bioshock* series has transitioned fully from the political to the metaphysical.

This multiverse-heavy setup to *Infinite*'s final DLC chapter also puts in place gameplay elements that are significant to explore from both a ludic perspective as well as from a gender power dynamic perspective. The gameplay and rules players experience throughout the primary *Infinite* game as well as the first "Burial at Sea" chapter are similar and rely on plentiful ammo, powerful vigors galore, and a significant amount of health to spare, whereas episode two strips most of these elements thereby relying on small amounts of ammo, vigors, and damage that can be absorbed. Controlling Elizabeth, a strong three-dimensional female video game character, as the primary protagonist in episode two seems on the surface to be a progressive representation and identification for players, but these gameplay changes reduce any positive impact. Not only is this player-controlled version of Elizabeth stripped of her dimension tearing powers, but she is also portrayed as significantly weaker than the male-controlled protagonists of the series. Whereas with Booker, in episode one, the citizens of Rapture are dispatched with the same relative ease as the full *Infinite* game, players in episode two must rely primarily on stealth with Elizabeth to avoid being easily killed by the same antagonists. Further research should explore this dynamic in more detail, as well as compare/contrast this episode to the brief moments in *Bioshock 2* where players controlled a Little Sister.

As the plot of episode two progresses, Elizabeth raises the prison Atlas occupies using a quantum particle, but he is not done using her. He decides she is the only one capable of telling him where the mysterious "ace in the hole" is—a powerful weapon to be used against Rapture's creator, Andrew Ryan. The key to Elizabeth's success in episode two is that before she actually made the decision to collapse in the quantum superposition, thereby losing her ability to access "all the doors" to the past, present, and future, she had previously had access to said doors. Her memories of what she saw, once she is jarred into recovering them, are what allow her to know where to find the "ace in the hole" that Atlas seeks. This "ace" is the crucial key to the final circular metaphysical connection in the *Bioshock* series. The "ace" is the activation phrase "would you kindly," and by telling it to Atlas, who is Frank Fontaine, Elizabeth sets into motion the entire plot of the original *Bioshock*. Moreover, it turns out that the character most associated with the *Bioshock* series' metaphysical musings, Elizabeth, was also responsible for many crucial events in the first game. These range from the Big Daddies' imprinting on the Little Sisters and patrolling Rapture to the eventual downfall of both Andrew Ryan and Frank Fontaine, the fanatical zealots. The circle is unbroken, and having Big Daddies, a symbol of control and oppression, and "ace" Jack, a character who represents a rumination about individuality and choice, both born from the quantum physics of Elizabeth serves to retroactively inject existential thought into the original series. Some of *Infinite*'s political discourse also ends up retroactively scrubbed, as a brief interdimensional sojourn Elizabeth takes to Columbia reveals that Comstock's primary political antagonist, the Vox Populi leader Daisy Fitzroy, was cognizant of her impending death and the ways it would serve the broader purpose of the quantum tearing Elizabeth. Everything from the connection between Rapture plasmids and Columbia vigors, and *Bioshock*'s scientist Suchong and *Infinite*'s inventor Fink, to how the ideological and political war between Andrew Ryan and Frank Fontaine comes to a head is retroactively given a quantum physics explanation through the events of "Burial at Sea: Episode 2."

The ending of *Infinite*-proper merely implied that the original *Bioshock* and its sequel were simply parallel versions of the same father-daughter relationship in conflict with a zealot. As parallel, the original two games retain their political discourse with their emphasis on the ridiculousness inherent in any absolutes. Once these games are placed within the loop of *Infinite*, they become a part of, and work in service of, quantum metaphysical musings thereby shifting the narrative from the historical to the existential. It is difficult to retain the importance of a historically based, counterfactual or not, critique when they directly result from an infinite self-generating loop of individualistic metaphysical problems.

ASSASSIN'S CREED (2007–PRESENT)

The *Assassin's Creed* series began in 2007 and Ubisoft has developed and published twelve games in the main series, along with a handful of ancillary games and other connected media properties. The series is complicated from a narrative perspective, as its foundational conceit is that present-day characters in the game can interactively experience the genetic memories of their ancestors, through a machine known as an "Animus." Essentially, the first *Assassin's Creed* (2007) approaches players as a nesting video game, with the real-world player controlling a character who is ultimately controlling a VR (virtual reality) version of their historical ancestors' lives. The present-day protagonist, which for the first game is Desmond Miles, is controlling the genetic memories of his ancestors, but he (or the real-world player) cannot change history; all he (they) can do is be more or less in "sync" with how the actual events unfolded for Desmond's ancestors. In the first game in the series, Desmond is experiencing the memories of his ancestor Altaïr through the cities of Jerusalem, Acre, and Damascus. However, since Altaïr did not die or fail in his various missions, if Desmond (or the real-life player) fails then the memory glitches and the Animus forces a restart of the memory sequence. The score and rewards Desmond (the player) gets after finishing a memory sequence depends on the level of synchronization they were able to achieve with the ancestor's lived genetic memory, so if Altaïr killed a certain person with a specific weapon then the player must do the same to achieve full synchronization and potentially unlock achievements, bonuses, and repressed memories.

These gameplay features and the way they are nested within the narrative structure are notable, but this series combines this all with real historical figures, real historical cities, and uses real historical events as a framework on which to base the series. Every *Assassin's Creed* game begins with the text "Inspired by historical events and characters. This work of fiction was designed, developed and produced by a multicultural team of various religious faiths and beliefs" hinting at the ways in which the creators of the series are attempting to inoculate its players against criticism for historical inaccuracies. There is an important distinction that should be made between a video game series like *Bioshock* and *Assassin's Creed*, as they resemble the definition of alternative history differently. While the *Bioshock* series appears to alter historical nexus points and watches them play out, the *Assassin's*

Creed series purports to exist in our experienced historical time line, just with events unfolding in the past that we are not aware happened. So as opposed to using history as a fork in the road from our current reality, the *Assassin's Creed* series takes a figure like Leonardo Da Vinci and spins his prolific inventions into fixing, designing, and creating weapons and tools for Ezio, the protagonist of *Assassin's Creed II* (2009), *Assassin's Creed: Brotherhood* (2010), and *Assassin's Creed: Revelations* (2011). Derek Theiss discusses this distinction while exploring the novel *The Da Vinci Code* (2003), saying that though this type of text is "properly an apocryphal history, uncovering an otherwise unknown history," it is "merely an inversion, rather than a negation, of the alternate history parabola" as it still modifies recognizable history (2014, 9). The one element of the present-day narrative that could tip the scales to make *Assassin's Creed* counterfactual, as opposed to apocryphal, would be the existence of the primary antagonist corporation, Abstergo, but this appears more to be a result of not wanting to make a real-world corporation like Google or Amazon appear evil than a result of counterfactual events in the games leading to a different present-day time line.

Working through the overarching series story will be helpful in this regard, to plot out the ways in which the apocryphal history can provide moments of historical inversion and open up potential encouragement of comparative and contemplative historical discourse and thought. This potential is primarily made possible through the employment of the overarching science fiction narrative in the present day, because otherwise the *Assassin's Creed* series would approach players more as atomized historical larks into various unrelated time periods. Instead, the series revolves around an apocryphal historic conflict between the titular Assassins and the Knights Templar, an actual group whose motivations are shaped to include world domination and control through the acquisition of the "Pieces of Eden" that have the power to control a person's thoughts and actions. In present day, the Knights Templar have developed Abstergo, a corporate conglomeration designed as a front to conceal their true motivations of eliminating the Assassin's, finding the Pieces of Eden, and as stated in *Assassin's Creed: Brotherhood* (2010) "shepherd those beneath us through life, even if force is required." One of their primary methods to achieve these goals is to subject modern-day people whose ancestors were in the Assassin brotherhood, sometimes unwittingly, to relive their genetic memories in the hopes of locating Pieces of Eden. Desmond Miles is not the first person they placed in the Animus; he is listed as "Subject 17," but he is the first that players control in the *Assassin's Creed* series debut. Desmond uncovers and synchronizes memory blocks, and when he successfully synchronizes with "Memory Block 7," he uncovers a glowing globe map of the locations of Pieces of Eden. Coming out of the Animus, Desmond learns that Abstergo is actually the Templars, and he is saved from execution by a lab tech named Lucy who is an undercover Assassin's agent. This catapults forward the modern-day story of Abstergo/Templars versus various members of the Assassins Brotherhood, including Desmond's father William. Desmond also experiences a "bleeding effect" where he has been in the Animus too long, and now the boundary between the past genetic memories and the present blur, and he acquires present-day Assassin abilities. This plot device serves to make an indirect connection between the game series and the theme of learning from history. The Animus bridge between the player's present day and the ancestral genetic memories is not often directly breached, but when it is there is also something to be gleaned. At the end of *Assassin's Creed II* (2009), Ezio, the ancestral Assassin that Desmond is controlling, brings an Apple of Eden to a glowing goddess-like character named Minerva who appears to be aware that Desmond (or the player themselves) is in control. She turns away from Ezio and looks directly at the player perspective, which confuses Enzio who says, "there's no one else here." Minerva says she has a message, a warning, that must be heeded by Desmond (the player). She says that other temples must be found, "built by those who knew to turn away from war." The message of world peace is clichéd; however, the method of delivery using a science fiction device to directly confront the present player with lessons from history is notable. It shows the critical historical potential of leveraging this specific combination of genre, subject, and medium. It also spurs Desmond on to his next series of missions in the next two games in the series, which combine with *Assassin's Creed II* to make up the "Ezio trilogy."

Several later entries in the *Assassin's Creed* series further blur this line between the modern-day protagonists and the real-world video game players, emphasizing this series' potential to encourage an adaptive and contemplative view of the past. Most of these increasingly blurry protagonist/player distinctions have to do with Abstergo's in-game narrative development of the Animus technology. The numbering gets a little off, but for the first five primary console games in the series, Desmond Miles is the protagonist who is able to use the Animus to explore his ancestors' memories, because of his genetic lineage. However, after his death at the end of *Assassin's Creed III* (2012), the fifth console game in the series, the focus shifts considerably. In *Assassin's Creed IV: Black Flag* (2013), Abstergo has created a division of their corporation called Abstergo Entertainment, that claims to just be interested in making films, which has developed the Animus further to allow for anyone to access genetic memories regardless of ancestry. This move is not only necessary from a narrative continuation of the series perspective once the decision was made to kill their genetically linked protagonist, but also serves to link the real-life video game players more in terms of identification, especially those players who might not align with Desmond's represented gender, ethnicity, or sexuality. If the argument is being made that the *Assassin's Creed* series provides opportunities for, and encouragement of, players to participate in an interactive version of apocryphal history that may lead to a more critical viewing of the past, then democratizing the access to these genetic memories only serves to strengthen this argument.

If democratizing historical memory access was the first step in connecting to real-life players, *Assassin's Creed Unity* (2014) makes the biggest leap by turning the Animus into a video game console called Helix. In the *Unity* narrative, the Helix console is sold by Abstergo to consumers to farm out their gameplay efforts to crowdsource the finding of Pieces of Eden, but the real-world players are given deep interactive connections as well. After a brief *Assassin's Creed Unity* title screen, the user interface switches to appear as if players are actually operating a Helix console. Narration introduces the console saying that "the past is not lost, the past is inside us" over animation of a double helix being formed by silver shards, going on to say they "have opened a window into the past, this is total immersion entertainment." The animation transitions to an actual Helix menu while saying, "With the press of a button, you will experience the most pivotal moments in history, all from the comfort of the Helix." The menu itself lists twelve thumbnail options, comprising both the stories the *Assassin's Creed* series has already tackled, such as Ezio's adventures entitled "Fear and Loathing in Florence," as well as ones that represent potential future series installments, such as "Jazz Age Junkies" (figure 8.1).

This menu is functional, as in the player can scroll over the different story options, but in the end the only actual option that can be selected in the upper left is the current installment entitled "The Tragedy of Jacques De Molay" as the others say "Locked" when you try to select them. This functions as a more immersive connection to the in-game narrative, as well as the gameplay of the Animus itself, allowing for the maximum encouragement of players to engage with history, even if it is apocryphal. The game narrative itself then blurs the player/protagonist line completely, by having a member of the Assassins, named Bishop, break through the Helix video game session and recruit the "Initiate," the actual real-world player, to help with a different memory, that of Arno Dorian who joins the Assassin Brotherhood in revolutionary France. This step to make the player and the modern-day protagonist one in the same works to get closer to realizing the interactive potentials that are contained within the overarching series Animus nesting story.

The Initiate player gameplay-narrative connection continues in the next entry, *Assassin's Creed Syndicate* (2015) set in Victorian London, but then *Assassin's Creed Origins* (2017) and *Assassin's Creed Odyssey* (2018) were

Assassin's Creed, Bioshock, *and Alternative Histories* 125

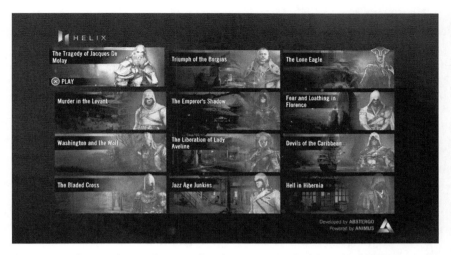

Figure 8.1 Players of *Assassin's Creed Unity* Are Greeted with a Simulated Interactive Environment from the In-game Narrative Console, Helix. *Source*: Assassin's Creed Unity (2014). Screenshot taken by author.

somewhat mundane in terms of their engagement with larger questions about player interactivity with the past, given that they both follow the newest protagonist facing off against Abstergo, named Layla. In the latest entry in the series, *Assassin's Creed Valhalla* (2020), there is a continuity with this overarching narrative about Layla and the Assassin's against the Templars and Abstergo, this time through the exploration of Eivor's genetic memories, a Viking raider in 873 Norway. The gameplay and Animus aesthetics are similar to the previous two entries, *Origins* and *Odyssey*, with one significant added player identification feature. After playing through a few cutscene heavy introduction sequences, Eivor is attacked by a wolf and the genetic memory begins glitching. The Animus operator tells Layla that she sees "two different data streams, overlapped in the same DNA." This leads to a menu option for players where they can either choose to play the female or male "Eivor memory-stream" or a third option where they can "let the ANIMUS choose" and it will "represent the stronger FEMALE or MALE memory-stream, depending on its current strength." An interesting idea, though the execution is somewhat muddled, as the only time the animus chooses to switch from female to male is during the Havi/Odin sequences as a form of nested memories of the female version of Eivor. It is no surprise that in a historically testosterone-soaked series, a commentary on gender-fluidity would be somewhat blunted, but the ability to change genders at any time and the few moments of changing mid-narrative should be highlighted for the ways they contribute to a more complicated gameplay experience and a compliment to the historical inversions present in the apocryphal histories of *Assassin's Creed*.

A brief note about the *Assassin's Creed* film adaptation (2016) is appropriate for the ways in which it does, and does not, use the science fiction tropes of the game series to connect with similar existential themes. Having both Cal and Aguilar played by the same actor, Michael Fassbender, the genetic ancestor connections are made as explicit as possible, and helps to connect its stated theme, "Your blood is not your own." The connections are made more innate as opposed to technologically driven, such as when Cal is first shown in present day he is drawing ancestors' memories on death row without ever having touched an Animus. Once inside the Animus, there are technological and visceral differences, as Cal is hooked to a rig that has him mirror the movements of the genetic memories in real life, even wearing the signature Assassin's wrist blades that belonged to his ancestor. The memories themselves are represented in smoky projections that surround the Animus space, and the film uses this effect and the mirrored motions to continually crosscut between the past and the present. The "bleeding effect," discussed in the game series after prolonged Animus exposure, occurs after just one session in the film, speaking to medium differences of considerably less screen time to develop these types of ideas as well as industrial economic constraints as it allows the film to stay in the less CGI-dependent present more often. By the end of the film, Cal synchronizes so fully that he breaks the Animus arm, but continues to be able to be in the memories of his ancestor. It is not that the Animus' and Cal's ancestral memories are not important, they are just decentralized compared to the video game series, which reduces the apocryphal history potentials for moments of historical inversion and comparative and contemplative historical thought.

CONCLUSION

What both the counterfactual video game series, *Bioshock*, and the apocryphal history video game series, *Assassin's Creed*, have in common is their encouragement of players to perform a "radical reframing of familiar events . . . capable of calling into question beginnings, endings, and everything in between" (Uricchio 2005, 335). Whether it is *Bioshock*'s use of familiar national heroes put in extremist environments, or it is *Assassin's Creed* shifting familiar historical figures and events to develop a hidden alternate history, both seek to provide opportunities for players to question the "inevitability of the here and now by showing the results of alteration" accepted historical facts (Hellekson 2001, 35). Where the two series differ might be in their execution of this encouragement over the course of the iterations.

With *Bioshock* the looping ending and DLC content served to potentially erase historical and political critique in its own series, or perhaps by placing an emphasis on the lack of interactive control that had become a hallmark of earlier games in the series. However, with *Assassin's Creed* the interactive potentials gained momentum as the series progressed, with many sequels enhancing the real-world video game players' connections to the protagonists' exploration of history.

Chapter 9

Interactive Existential Science Fiction

As was explored in the previous chapter, the existential science fiction trend has flourished across media, including interactive video games. The ways in which this type of complex video game has proliferated in recent years can be attributed to a myriad of factors, not the least of which could be the medium's iterative technological development cycles. Much in the same way that early film and television were simply not capable of containing the same level of complexity that contemporary versions of these media can, the video game has only relatively recently reached technological and artistic levels commensurate with the leaps forward in other media. *Pong* (1972) could not achieve the same complexity that a game released today is capable of reaching. If the previous chapter examined the existential science fiction video game's ability to provoke a contemplative view of history through counterfactual and apocryphal representations, then this chapter will explore the confluence of interactivity and existential thought. An argument will be made that the contemporary video game is capable of leveraging its interactivity, through metacommentaries and destabilizing gameplay elements, in service of enhanced levels of complex philosophical musings about humanity and existence. To demonstrate this interactive trend, I will analyze two contemporary science fiction video games, *SOMA* (2015) and *Death Stranding* (2019), to show this trend and how it differs from other media in the same historical existential science fiction media trend.

Both of these titles contains structural gameplay elements that realize the ideal interactive environment to connect to Amanda Lagerkvist's idea that "digital media are *existential media*" as they offer "new spaces for the exploration of existential themes and the profundity of life" (2017, 97; emphasis in original). Lagerkvist seeks to explain how "classic existential issues have become more and more entwined with our digital lives" and that "we seem to be, to speak in Heideggerian terms, *thrown* into our digital human existence," which leads to a situation where "our sense of time, memory, space, self-hood, sociality, and death are implicated" (2017, 97; emphasis in original). If this all seems heavy for interactive video games, then consider that the games discussed in this chapter will tackle everything from the nature of consciousness, humanity, identity, free will, and death. And these topics are not explored allegorically, or symbolically, but head-on and overtly. Lagerkvist helps in this definitional regard as well, arguing that "existential media analysis also needs to account for—and reconcile its ontological claims with—the thrownness of the digital human condition" and that this

> thrownness implies being faced with a world where we are precariously situated in a particular place, at a particular historical moment, and among a particular crowd with the inescapable task of tackling our world around us and to make it meaningful. (2017, 97)

What this chapter will take from these methodological suggestions is that the digital interactive video games must vault their players into a world where existentiality cannot be ignored or unmoored from its particular ontological positioning. I argue this is achieved by the destabilizing gameplay elements and meta-commentary on the nature of gaming itself. The mechanism in place is one similar to Bertolt Brecht's alienation effect, where actors are

> playing in such a way that the audience was hindered from simply identifying itself with the characters in the play. Acceptance or rejection of their actions and utterances was meant to take place on a conscious plane, instead of, as hitherto, in the audience's subconscious. (1964, 91)

By giving players an unfamiliar, and sometimes uncomfortable, gaming experience, these games allow focus on the existential thematic elements and "enable sense-making in relation to the precariousness of life and the basics of 'why are we here'" (Lagerkvist 2017, 98).

Much of the unfamiliar gameplay experience comes from the breaking of player expectations, including the assumed roles of antagonists and protagonists. As noted in chapter eight, a video game without any form of personified antagonism is rare given the medium and industry constraints. Even *Candy Crush* (2012) has villains. However, both games discussed in detail in this chapter complicate the protagonist/antagonist relationship, with *SOMA*'s "WAU" whose goal is to save mankind and *Death Stranding*'s BTs that may just be looking for human connection. There are other notable examples worth mentioning briefly here, as they stand as indie-game precursors that could be said to be influential in their subverting expectations through destabilizing the player experience. *The Stanley Parable* (2011), developed and published by Galactic Cafe, is an influential independent video game that puts the player's interactive actions at the forefront of its narrative. Players control office employee 427, Stanley, as he is asked to make decisions that either go with or against what a narrator is telling the player must be done. With multiple endings that often directly address the gamer and the gameplay, it is a game that is an interactive meta-commentary but not an existential one. *Inside* is a 2016 side-scrolling game developed and published by Playdead about a future dystopian society where scientists conduct experiments on mind-controlled humans, and players control a boy trying to escape their grasp. Semantically, the science fiction connections are not as explicit as in the case of *SOMA*, but the dystopian setting and the science of mind control and human experimentation seem to qualify inclusion in the genre even if tangentially, much like *Eternal Sunshine of the Spotless Mind* (2004) appears at once to be science fiction and also indie mumblecore. Syntactically, the existential exploration revolves around the connection between what it is to be human in an increasingly controlled world and the gamer itself. The game, like those in this chapter, leverages its narrative and gameplay to make a meta-commentary on those playing the interactive media text. Playdead previously released a game entitled *Limbo* (2010) that followed the same side-scrolling gameplay engine, but none of the science fiction elements beyond a few mind-controlling worms. Players guide an unnamed boy through a myriad of deadly puzzles, and are confronted with the interactive idea that they likely cannot make it through the game without failing, as the "developers describe Limbo as a trial-and-death game" (Hatfield 2011). All of these examples, among others, began to prove to the video game industry and players alike that expectations were made to be broken and that this was a medium adept at presenting deep philosophical content enhanced by an interactive version of Brecht's alienation effect.

SOMA (2015)

Deriving its names from the Greek word for "body," *SOMA* is a 2015 first-person survival horror video game created by Frictional Games that follows the story of Simon Jarrett and the PATHOS-II underwater research facility, the last vestiges of "humanity" on a postapocalyptic Earth. Simon suffers brain trauma from a car accident in 2015 and opts to have his brain scanned by a doctoral student so that he can "build a computer model of it, then bombard it with stimuli" in an attempt to "quickly iterate your treatment plan until its fully optimized." The player as Simon sits in the researcher's brain scan chair, makes a joke about cameras stealing one's soul, then there is some static across the gameplay screen accompanied by a white flash, and Simon wakes up in the year 2104 on the PATHOS-II. The implication is that the version of Simon from 2015 went on living his life after the scan, and this version is a copy of his memories, consciousness, and identity now booted up in the future. To this copied version of Simon, no time has passed with a direct continuity of consciousness despite the nearly 100-year gap in time. What follows is a deep exploration of ideas of humanity, consciousness, identity, memory, and existence itself, through encounters with robots that believe they are human, other brain scanned people, and transfers of consciousness. The Frictional Games Press Kit self-describes *SOMA* as an "unsettling story about identity, consciousness, and what it means to be human" (2021). *SOMA* begins with a quote from Philip K. Dick, "Reality is that which, when you stop believing in it, doesn't go away," and works through the idea of the persistence and definition of consciousness as something that exists at levels we do not always consider, but leverages the tropes of interactive first-person video games to force players to contemplate them anyway.

Simon flashes into 2104 unaware of anything that transpired since 2015, as he stumbles through the PATHOS-II research facility looking for clues as to how he got there. As he walks, we get the first idea that Simon may not be who he once was, with his field of vision, and ours given the first-person perspective, glitching out and showing static. As he explores PATHOS-II, Simon learns that he can access the final moments of an entity's consciousness by touching them. This will later be named "data mining" and is connected to "black boxes" that monitored all humans vitals at PATHOS-II. Simon touches a robot hanging on the wall and hears its final interaction with a human who does not enjoy its newfound humanity, as they are heard saying, "Yeah, you're creepy as hell, so I'm gonna shut you down," as the recording cuts to static. Early in the game, Simon encounters a broken-looking robot on the floor connected to a console by two tendril-like hoses. When he disconnects them, the machine tells him to stop and asks him in a trembling feminine sounding human voice, "Why? I was okay, I was happy," before going dark and appearing to die. Players have to perform this action to progress the game, and they are made to confront the destruction of a seemingly conscious being that may not look human, but acted and sounded like one. This is not the only time during *SOMA* that players are forced to unplug a seemingly sentient being in order to restore stability or operating capacity to a part of PATHOS-II, with the task becoming increasingly pointed when Simon encounters what appears to be a cyborg being kept alive by an artificial lung attached to the Upsilon Shuttle Station B. Simon must detach the power to this lung, effectively killing the pleading cyborg with a human head. Here, *SOMA* is leveraging interactivity to explore existential questions of consciousness and humanity by forcing players to perform these actions if they want to progress in the game.

When Simon proceeds to approach a robot that has its bottom half torn apart, he asks it "What are you?" to which it matters-of-factly replies in a masculine northeast accented voice, "Are you blind? It's me Carl. Carl Semken." *SOMA* uses security cameras on the heads of robots, with their accompanying red lights, to introduce some potential mystery as to whether those talking are simply on the other end of some video feed, though players learn through these interactions that is not the case at all and the robots themselves talk and feel and think that they are human. Carl says he has been "knocked out on the floor," confirming he is not a disembodied voice somewhere else, and when Simon asks him if he is human, Carl responds by tapping his head and saying, "Did my body give it away . . . yeah, I'm human." Simon does not understand and asks Carl where he is, to which Carl says, "I'm right here. See me waving?," as he moves his robot arm back and forth. After having to tell him a third time, in case players did not get it by now, Carl admonishes that Simon is really "hung up on appearances." A key moment occurs after this exchange, as Carl describes how he got hurt while remote piloting a robot UH (Universal Helper). Simon chimes in to clarify that Carl was remote piloting a robot, to which Carl obliviously responds, "Robots are too unaware to deal with some stuff. Intuition doesn't grow on motherboards." This sequence establishes the existential facts of the robots of PATHOS-II, which unabashedly believe they are actual human beings, not robots with artificial intelligence or even implanted consciousness from previously living humans. However, Simon later discovers Carl's deceased human body, confirming that a copy of Carl's mind is trapped in the UH unit that he just encountered.

SOMA uses these moments of perception versus reality to challenge the nature of existence, and how our senses can present a view of the world that does not align with reality. Simon faces the first challenge to his assumed reality when a chamber floods with him in it. If his senses of who and what he is were correct, it would be natural to fear he would drown, but as the water fills the chamber the audio of his breathing changes to that of a respirator. Simon does not understand, says, "How is this possible," and then holds his human hands in front of his face, which is the player's view as well given the first-person perspective. Suddenly, the hands flash and glitch and are replaced with gloved diver suit hands. Simon's subjective perception of his hands was that of a normal human, until that perception was challenged with the reality of the water around him.

Simon's progress through *SOMA* is spurred on by his contact with the first seemingly live human interaction over the radio, Catherine Chun at Site Lambda. She talks with Simon over various radios and guides him through areas of PATHOS-II to reach the Lambda site via a shuttle and then a maintenance hatch. When he arrives, he is distressed to see a half-broken computer screen on the ground instead of a human that resembles the picture of her that appeared when he talked with her. Simon says, "No, not you too. I was really hoping you were human," to which she responds, "Don't let the circuitry fool you, I was human once." The game really begins to put Simon in a similar existential position when he laments to Catherine that he is worried that he is the last human left, and she asks him, "Have you looked at yourself lately? You're a walking, talking diving suit with some electronics slapped on for good measure." Simon temporarily moves on from this existential crisis, but not before he lets slip that he does not want to "be" this anymore, speaking to a growing awareness of his artificial humanity. Catherine asks Simon to put her chip into his Omnitool v2.5, which contains the onboard "A.I. Helper JaneTM" that you can modify with "fully customized tolls and assistants" via the Omnitool Chip Installer terminals. Once the Catherine chip is installed, Helper Jane is replaced with Catherine and Simon now carries her consciousness around with him. This new found mobility is not without its downsides, as she seems to only be conscious when she is plugged into a console, and every time Simon does plug her in she reacts to being startled awake in a new environment. When plugged into a unit on the way to Theta station, she remarks that "it's really disconcerting popping in and out of existence like that." The implication is that she has the perception of an unbroken continuity of consciousness, but in reality there are time and space gaps. She also makes sure to repeatedly remind the player/Simon not to "forget to take me with you," which serves as a practical reminder for players as Simon needs the Omnitool but is also a hint at the existential questions *SOMA* will ask throughout as copies of consciousness are made, discarded, and/or sent into space. She explains earlier that her purpose on PATHOS-II was a project called ARK designed to "save all the people on the station as brain scans and put them into an artificial world" with the intention to launch them into space, which is when a comet hit Earth destroying the surface world. Catherine notes that she does not even know if the human version of her that scanned their brain is still alive, but dismisses it as a "weird thought."

This "weird thought" is the central existential question of *SOMA*, what does it mean to be a conscious human? In interviews about the ARK project, one subject, Mark Sarang, remarks about the great value of the project as a way that "we can go on living through the reality of continuity." This concept of what the digital copy of one's consciousness would perceive, that being an unbroken sense of continuity is vital for its feelings of authentic humanity. Other science fiction media that deals with this concept of digital copies of memories, such as *Blade Runner* (1982) and *Westworld* (2016–present), similarly place emphasis on the unbroken continuity as the cornerstone to making the artificial entity feel human. However, the implication of continuity as humanity foundation is predicated on the perception of authenticity, which is threatened when confronted with even the idea of other existing versions of the same consciousness.

An overarching AI exists on PATHOS-II called the Warden Unit (or WAU), which Catherine describes as a cancer as it invades every part of the stations. Simon asks whether the WAU is the reason for all of the robot-human consciousness across the stations, to which she replies that "it's not directed with purpose" and again asks him to not worry about it right now. Later, when Simon asks her why she thinks the WAU made him, she reveals that the "WAU had a range of assignments, but they all spring from one single idea: preserve humanity." WAU's strategy for preserving humanity, implanting consciousnesses into robots, and corrupting humans and their corpses in grotesque manners serve as the primary antagonists/enemies in *SOMA*, but even here the expectations of players are subverted. Categorized as survival horror, taking place under the sea, and dealing with existential themes, *SOMA* sounds like it would have gameplay and/or fight mechanics in line with the *Bioshock* series (2007–2013); however, there is no mechanism to fight and defeat these enemies. No weapons to speak of at all, just the need to distract and avoid enemies to move on to a new location. In fact, the only moment Simon gets ahold of something akin to a gun is when he is forced to shoot a sentient floating robot multiple times with a stun gun as it tells you "that hurts." Simon reflects on this encounter to Catherine and how it was not right because "he was talking" and seemed "sincere, present." Players have to reflect on the idea that the only time they shot anything in *SOMA* it was peaceful and seemed human. He goes on to tell Catherine that it is "beginning to sink in" that he is "a robot" even though his brain keeps trying to "suppress" this fact. Catherine keeps telling him to not worry about it, and keeps him task-oriented, but he says he "can't help thinking about what we've become. It's clear that we're no longer human, but then how can I feel like Simon?" The final enemy encounter in *SOMA* is no more antagonistic, as players must decide whether to destroy the WAU, not by fighting it but by simply touching a button on their controllers that makes Simon infect the WAU with "structural gel." Regardless of which decision players make, the WAU creator, Dr. Johan Ross, will attempt to kill Simon, but in either case will be unsuccessful without a fight from the player. *SOMA* is about making players question their role in interactive media by subverting the assumed goals/gameplay of the genre, all in service of the broader question of humanity and consciousness.

The survival or coexistence of consciousness copies becomes an important issue to deal with or overcome, given the setup of *SOMA*. When Simon encounters a broken robot with the consciousness of a woman named Robin

Bass, she invokes the idea of trying to achieve as close to an unbroken continuity of consciousness as possible, having apparently killed herself shortly after being brain scanned so that one single version could live on in the ARK. The post-scan suicides were not part of the plan, but those who were scanned kept doing so, causing the ARK project to be put in jeopardy. Catherine describes this ARK as a "perfectly immersive" environment that is "like real life, but slightly better" that "attached to a probe, fueled by solar panels it could survive for thousands of years." Simon is coming around to the idea that this task is saving "the final remains of humanity," and though it is all digital it "feels worth doing." The implication of these two thoughts combined, the final remains and the worthiness of the task, is that if this is all that is left of humanity then it is a noble task, but that is only because there is no authentic version left on Earth. Simon comes across a terminal with recordings of his former human self from 2015 after the brain scan, and players learn the treatment did not work for his brain damage and that he ultimately died but donated the brain scan to future research. This is the moment that Simon knows the full story of his current condition: "No magic or time travel needed. I was here all along waiting for someone to shove a picture of my brain into a suit and hit the power button." Players also have the option to have Simon delete these recordings, and though there is no effect on the gameplay to do so, the decision hints at the philosophical questions underpinning *SOMA*. Players are faced with a similar delete decision when Simon must load the scan of Brandon Wan to obtain a "security cypher," and doing so brings their unbroken continuity back online to the moment right after their scan occurred. The stress level causes the simulation to shut down, effectively killing this version of Brandon again. Simon tries again with a beach simulation loaded, but Brandon's consciousness recognizes that it is "not real" and shuts down again. Simon then copies over the "Scan Room" environment, because it is noted to provide "Better continuation," but to ultimately get the cypher he has to couple this with knowledge of who Brandon was because "as soon as he starts to doubt, we've lost him." This gameplay sequence is very similar in setup to the *Black Mirror* episode "White Christmas" (2014), where a virtual version of someone's consciousness is able to be repeatedly rebooted from a save point until the desired result is achieved. Much like with Simon's 2015 recordings, players have the option to delete Brandon Wan's data (effectively his consciousness) or to leave it to languish and potentially be used at some later time by the WAU, further deepening the connection between gameplay and the question of coexisting consciousnesses.

Simon learns that he is not like the other robots with brain scan copies loaded onto them, but instead loaded into a deceased body through a "cortex chip." He is not happy to learn this, saying, "I'm half a dead person," but Catherine assures him that this is the "best of both worlds. A sound mind in a sound body." But this is not the last body that Simon will inhabit, as he must eventually have his brain copied into a "power suit" with a dead body inside that can withstand the increased pressure of the water depth he must go to, which spurs the most significant decision whether to delete a conscious entity or not. The issue that Simon does not realize is that this is a copy, not a transfer of consciousness. Once Simon's brain is copied over to the power suit body, the version of him in the diver suit keeps on living, with two unbroken continuities of consciousness now existing simultaneously. Power suit Simon hears the diver suit version of himself in the other room "still talking," because that version thinks the transfer did not actually work. Power suit Simon is disgusted, but recognizes that they are going to leave diver suit Simon here alone to die, so Catherine sets up a switch next to him that will "drain his battery" so he would "die within a minute." Players must confront this interactive existential decision head-on, as the switch is right next to the still breathing diver suit Simon. If players push the button, his breathing slows to a stop and somber music plays.

A subsequent sequence in *SOMA* where Simon is descending to retrieve the ARK forces players to confront the existential questions that are bothering Simon, because there is nothing interactive to do during this journey other than to listen and wait. Simon considers his existential place among the different versions of himself, asking Catherine about afterlife potentials and whether "heaven is full of redundant copies of the same people"? He also now further questions the futility of what they are doing when "all the people still left are digital copies trapped in computers at the bottom of the sea." All of this while players just wait for the next interactive moment, contributing to *SOMA*'s meta-commentary on the player's role in an existential video game. The interactive existential moments and decisions continue, as Simon reaches the Tau site where the ARK is kept. Simon encounters Sarah Lindwall, the "first normal living human" he has seen, and they both soon figure out that she is the "last living human on the planet." But Sarah is clearly sick, and is hooked up to machines keeping her alive in exactly the same way as some of the sentient machines Simon has encountered. So when she asks Simon to kill her, the progression of decisions that players of *SOMA* must make takes a decidedly human step forward. Players can push a button on a life support machine next to Sarah, and she asks if you will stay with her as she dies, lamenting, "What a crazy thing this was, life" and telling Simon to make sure he sends the people in the ARK "to the stars" as she dies.

Once in the Phi site, Catherine and Simon finally have the ARK and are prepared to launch it into space, but not before players have their interactive expectations flipped one last time. Up to this point, every time Simon's consciousness has been copied into a new body/time, players have followed with the new version, with the game even asking them to kill their former selves. This time, when Catherine copies their consciousnesses into the ARK as it launches into space, players are "left behind" in the previous power suit Simon version. Their unbroken continuity of play matches Simon's unbroken continuity of consciousness, only this time it does not progress with the new copied version. Catherine calls it losing "the coin toss" saying it is "just like the man who died in Toronto a hundred years ago," but that the versions that won "are both safe on the ARK, be happy for them." A video game is classically about progression, but here, in its final moments, *SOMA* subverts this expectation, hammering home its existential questions about humanity and what constitutes existence. Are players still playing the "same" Simon they have been along, or was that changed back during the 2015 to 2104 or the diver to power suit switch? Players are given a view into the other versions of Catherine and Simon who were copied onto the ARK, in an idyllic virtual world presiding over a destroyed Earth in a satellite, but this crucially comes as a post-credits sequence so players are given the time and interactive space to fully contemplate these questions. *SOMA* leverages its science fiction semantic elements as well as the interactive expectations of its players to fully explore the syntactic existential themes of existence, humanity, consciousness, and identity.

DEATH STRANDING (2019)

Hideo Kojima is responsible for some of the most cerebral, complicated, and genre-bending video games of all time, including the *Metal Gear* series (1987–present), *Snatcher* (1988), and *P.T.* (2015). *Death Stranding* is no different, with its unique gameplay mechanisms, hauntingly existential storyline, and use of geography as an atmospheric element. Much of what can be said about *Death Stranding* would surround its connections to the past in a nostalgic manner, however, that is not the focus of this book so will be mostly saved for a later exploration of the video game. Instead, the focus of this analysis of *Death Stranding* will be on the ways in which the game positions humanity's existence and the potentials of an afterlife, and uses these elements to destabilize the assumed gameplay mechanics and genre elements often present in postapocalyptic science fiction video games. Even describing *Death Stranding* is difficult, and complicated, so do not worry if its various plot points make little sense, I will focus on their interactive implications and connections to the existential musings of the game. Korine Powers, presenting on the game, describes it succinctly:

> In rough outline, *Death Stranding* is a cooperative single player haunted stealth shooter and walking simulator. You play through *Death Stranding* as Sam

Porter Bridges, a delivery man who hauls packages across the dystopian remains of the United Cities of America following a supernatural nuclear-equivalent event that has brought the dead in immediate, disastrous contact with the living. Sam delivers physical goods with the help of his Bridge Baby, or BB, a prenatal infant housed in a pod that is wirelessly connected to the womb of their brain-dead still-mother, while simultaneously convincing the few Americans left alive to join the Chiral Network, a powerful internet connected by the beaches that unite the living world and the afterlife. (2020)

Complicated, to be sure, but the elements within this game and description are at the heart of the interactive dissonance that players feel with *Death Stranding*, which in turn keep the focus on the existential elements contained within.

First off, the notion of a cooperative single player game is already somewhat oxymoronic, but is exactly how the gameplay operates, as players never encounter other avatars controlled by other synchronous players. Instead, players find markers, items, and lockers left by other players who have placed them in the same location at a different time. So if there is a particularly difficult mountain range to traverse, you may come across a ladder left by a previous player to help you on your way. Discussing this gameplay structure, Russ Frushtick calls *Death Stranding* a "wholly unique open-world adventure with asynchronous cooperative multiplayer that allows me to feel like I'm part of a community, building a world from scratch" (2019). Second, the concept of a walking simulator is already a destabilizing phrase in the interactive world of video games, as players may naturally take for granted the concept of walking in a game. How often is walking as simple as tilting the analog controller stick forward? Instead, *Death Stranding* complicates this process by forcing players to account for weight distribution of Sam's loaded gear and giving them balance controls in their controller trigger buttons. Kojima recognizes the alienating effect of this choice, saying that the players he watched test this walking dynamic "don't get it at first. But when they really start playing, just walking is really fun in the space" (Juba 2019). What Kojima calls fun is literally destabilizing the gameplay experience, as the expected motions of gaming are denatured. For players, this makes the very act of traversing the game world's geography, which is the primary gameplay structure of *Death Stranding*, something that must be paid attention to constantly. Vehicles exist in the game, and they do make traversal a lot easier and quicker, but they are not introduced until players have been thoroughly exposed to the walking simulator, and they are not without their own alienating effects as they frequently break down, need charging, and often rely on the asynchronous cooperative gameplay to be truly useful. Geography and balance as gameplay is highlighted in the first real delivery mission of the game, where Sam must transport the deceased body of the president of the United Cities of America, Bridget Strand, on his back to an incinerator. The mission is difficult because of the unfamiliar controls, and works as a walking tutorial, but as Sam gets into the open wilderness and a song title, "Bones" by LOW ROAR, appears and hauntingly begins playing while you walk, it is clear that *Death Stranding* wants players to connect this moment of unnatural gameplay to its emotional existential core.

In this sequence where players are transporting the president's dead body to an incinerator before it causes an explosive "voidout," you encounter your first Beached Thing, or BT. These beings are part of the titular *Death Stranding*, as they are stranded deceased who failed to cross over to the afterlife from The Beach. Initially invisible to humans, BTs appear as wispy black smoke/tar that seem to be attracted to living things, which they consume triggering a voidout explosion. Deceased humans, like the body of the President that Sam is hauling, must be burned before they necrotize into this tar-like substance and become a BT. When encountering these beings, which they can sense are in the area through their BBs and their suits, players must either stealthily avoid them or attack them with weapons infused with Sam's blood. These weapons work because Sam is a "repatriate," able to return endlessly from death, an obvious meta-nod to respawning in video games and giving his bodily fluids anti-BT powers. The relationship between the BBs, Sam and his bodily fluids, the BTs, and humanity's existence are the crux of *Death Stranding*'s existential exploration. Sam's BB, eventually named Lou, is literally attached to him "via cybernetic umbilical cord" (Powers 2020), and he must comfort Lou to build their connection. Powers notes the co-opting of pregnancy thematics throughout, saying, "While much of *Death Stranding*'s world dwells on life and death more broadly, Sam's story is largely about parenthood and delivery" (2020). Powers goes on to argue that it is "ultimately Sam's body, encoded with the impact and danger of his labors and deliveries, that is productive, connective and playable" (2020). Going far beyond the standard science fiction video game fare, where the protagonist has some innate or acquired ability to fight the enemies such as in the *Infamous* series (2009–2014), *Death Stranding* uses the attached BB and the blood of Sam to avoid and fight entities stranded between the living and the dead so they can traverse a pastoral countryside in order to reconnect an isolated postapocalyptic people.

Above all, *Death Stranding*, buttressed by its cooperative solo campaign, appears to be about connections with ourselves and those around us. Sam embodies the tug and pull of loneliness versus connections, as he literally treks across the country to reconnect its people but his body is "notably covered in handprints, as his severe aphenphosmphobia, fear of being touched, produces a handprint shaped rash or bruise on his body" (2020). Kojima notes this dichotomy, saying, "You're all alone playing the game, and you're trying to connect this fractured society by yourself. The world is beautiful, but you're small, just a tiny speck. You feel hopeless and helpless and powerless. You feel so lonely" (Gault 2019). This desire for connectedness extends to those we have lost, with Matthew Gault stating that "Kojima's personal take is that the dead are never truly gone from our lives," and Kojima adding that "you just can't see them, but you're connected" (2019). This invisible presence is echoed in the asynchronous cooperative gameplay, with Kojima adding that when you see items left behind it can remind you that other players are there even if you cannot see them, and "just knowing that, you won't feel alone anymore" (Gault 2019).

The philosophy of Kojima Productions, *Death Stranding* being their first produced title, mirrors much of this game's existential ethos. They have a mascot, named "Ludens," and a motto, "From Sapiens to Ludens," taken from "Dutch historian and cultural theorist Johan Huizinga, who claimed that the act of playing (ludus) is what makes human beings human—and that it predates culture" (Tani and Nitta 2017). Kojima himself wrote a poem to go along with this worldview, also entitled "From Sapiens to Ludens," which says that "'Playing' is not a pastime, it is the primordial basis of imagination and creation" and "through the invention of play, our new evolution awaits" (Kojima, n.d.). Hideo Kojima, his production company, and their game *Death Stranding* have a commonality whereby the expectations of the medium and genre are leveraged only to be subverted in service of deeper philosophical meaning. *Death Stranding* is a science fiction stealth shooter video game, which as a description carries a lot of assumptions about how it will play and what level of complex thought to expect. However, through the denaturing controls, the unconventional cooperative gameplay, and the existential thematic content, *Death Stranding*, presents a player experience thoroughly and deeply about human existence and connectivity. There is plenty more to discuss within *Death Stranding*, as this analysis went the whole time without even mentioning the concept of "Timefall." This game is existential, but it is also nostalgic in a way that should be explored in detail in another work.

CONCLUSION

The argument put forth in this chapter is not, as it might seem, that video games are finally technologically complex enough to tell meaningful stories. This is true from a relative perspective, given that the industry itself is less than half the age of the film industry, but there is much more going on with *SOMA* and *Death Stranding*. These games are simply representative of a medium that can capitalize on its interactivity in ways that encourage deep philosophical thought. As Amanda Lagerkvist said, we are "thrown into our digital human existence," and we should come to terms with the fact that "digital media are *existential media*" offering "both new existential predicaments, and at once new spaces for the exploration of existential themes and the profundity of life" (2017, 97; emphasis in original). Combine this digital existential nature with the science fiction genre, with its ability to manifest these abstract concepts in a generic environment historically about the exploration of new frontiers and ideas, and you get a powerful set of media texts that ask their players to contemplate what it means to exist, think, play, and connect as human beings.

Concluding Remarks

It is my hope that when you take a look at the overarching history of science fiction media, and the existential potentials within, that you see a series of fascinating examples of previous eras where there existed some deep and influential philosophical content focused on who we are as humans. Although this content did not always prove to be immediately influential, it laid the groundwork for existential philosophical content to expand and flourish at various times throughout media history. Then, in comparison, it is my hope that I have made a cogent enough argument that over the past decade or so there has been a marked increase in the depth and consistency of the science fiction genre's engagement with these existential musings, across all media. This increase has created a cultural cluster of existential science fiction content that provides a unique outlet for explorations of what it means to be human.

The science fiction genre itself contains more than its share of inherent existential potential, given its consistent focus on the movement of technology, exploration, and human abilities beyond what is currently achievable. When there is a subgenre literally titled "the overreacher," then it is clear that the genre is about pushing boundaries. Even with this inherent potential, there are moments and eras within science fiction media that seem to eschew the existential in exchange for the action-heavy plotline that at best can be described as allegorically philosophical, but is more likely just designed to exploit the economic appeal of the genre. It often seemed that when an existentially noteworthy film, television show, or other media text came along, the elements that were most commonly copied were not the syntactic philosophical elements, but instead the semantic elements like spaceships and alien invasions. Never was this more evident in the transition from the earlier science fiction films, like *Destination Moon* (1950), that paved the way for a much more exploitational version of the genre once the economic benefit of cheaper content proved to equal larger profit margins.

However, in its moments of philosophical depth, whether fleeting or part of the contemporary cultural cluster, science fiction media proved that it is at its best when it leverages its inherent generic potentials to "reconcile man with the unknown" (Sobchack 1997, 63). *Metropolis* (1927) demonstrated that existential exploration could be achieved without saying a word. The 1950s showed that there could still be allegorical content that bleeds through even the most fervently exploitational economical media environment. Films like *2001: A Space Odyssey* (1968), *Solaris* (1972), and *Blade Runner* (1982) proved that clusters of this type of existential content could build from each other, even if their broader influence would not be fully borne out immediately. The 1980s and 1990s made clear that once the cycle turns more action-focused it is difficult to break out of this trend, with Bradley Schauer arguing that these decades contained an "unabashed embrace of old SF tropes like robots, space battles, and grotesque aliens" (2016, 2). The late 1990s and early 2000s showed some promising examples of clearly existential science fiction content, such as *Contact* (1997) and *Eternal Sunshine of the Spotless Mind* (2004), but their economic and critical successes proved unable to inspire a cluster like the one that has flourished over the past decade. Then, along comes *Gravity* (2013), a film about rebirth, loss, and humanity made in a traditionally antagonistic-heavy genre, to either serve as the financial success story catalyst for the existential science fiction subgenre or was simply the first in a cyclical trend of science fiction media toward the philosophical. In either case, seeing how many other media artifacts followed this model of deep existential musings, often with nary an antagonist beyond nature and physics, is remarkable.

From *Interstellar* to *Arrival* to *Ad Astra*, if the movement of the science fiction genre toward the philosophical existed solely in the film medium it would have been interesting in its own right. However, the contemporary cluster of existential science fiction is potentially most interesting because of the breadth of media it flourishes in, from traditional areas like films and literature to more novel areas like television and video games. Much of this can be attributed to the ways in which media companies themselves have become multimedia conglomerates who seek to maximize their owned properties' reach. If a property like X-Men can be considered existential, for its exploration of human abilities and evolution, then it only makes sense in today's convergent media environment for that specific existential science fiction property to extend from film to television to streaming services to video games. It is in this fracturing and expansion of the media environment that trends can flourish more quickly than in previous eras. In fact, there was a lot of consideration to include a chapter in this book dedicated solely to existential science fiction on streaming platforms, which would have likely included examples like *The Cloverfield Paradox* (2018) and *The Midnight Sky* (2020) on Netflix and series like *Raised by Wolves* (2020–present) and *Made for Love* (2021–present) on HBO Max. Not only does the potentials in this type of media expansion speak to the ever-shifting ground on which all of these dynamics are built, but also to the potentials for how a cultural cluster forms or disappears. This is not to say that the only way to create a broad cultural cluster like existential science fiction is through conglomeration, especially given that the majority of the discussed texts in this book were derived from stand-alone properties. However, the very existence of a media environment that is so synergistic would imply that once a trend proves successful that its potential to permeate large cultural swaths has increased.

Throughout these different media, it is noteworthy that often the existential science fiction contemporary text carries with it a challenge to the accepted characteristics of the genre and medium in which it is made. From the lack of antagonism in a film genre often steeped in battles with aliens to interactive video games that force players to question their agentive motivations, the questioning of human existence often comes with a complementary questioning of media consumption itself. It is possible this kind of avant-garde medium challenging is simply the result of the already challenging philosophical content, as the type of media makers willing to push the intellectual boundaries may already be attuned to questioning consumption practices as well. Or there may be something inherent about the existential science fiction media text that specifically complements meta media commentaries and structural disruptions. It will be worth keeping an eye on whether the existential science fiction media text eventually becomes a fully codified subgenre, as opposed to the cyclical cultural cluster that it is at the moment, and if that codification would entail a jettisoning of the meta media elements.

The changing connection between the boundary pushing existential content and the meta media commentaries is just one of the elements to watch with the existential science fiction media text. As with all mediated cycles and genres, the trend line of this subgenre is likely to continue evolving and may ebb as quickly as it began flowing. Since the writing of this book, there have probably been examples released that either prove the existential science fiction media text is continuing to grow or is making way for another cyclical trend toward a more action- and antagonist-focused version of the genre, as was seen in the late 1950s. Regardless of which direction the genre is headed, we can use this contemporary cluster of science fiction media that was allowed the opportunity to deeply examine the nature of human existence, and ask ourselves why was the media environment so hospitable to these kinds of texts at this given moment. Was it really just a matter of success begetting opportunity, and once the successes no longer outweigh the losses there will be a regression of existential content? Or was there some deeper cultural need for existential exploration that the science fiction genre was uniquely adept at tapping into right now? Future research into this trend, and others like it, would likely do a more thorough job of looking at the media convergence factors that led to the existential science fiction trend to thrive across all connected media conglomerate outlets. Furthermore, future researchers could use this trend to help identify future generic cycles and move toward or away from philosophical explorations.

The future of existential science fiction media may be unknown, but their history and present are a fascinating look at what happens when the inherent potentials of a genre are realized to create explorations about the nature of our existence as humans. Abstract concepts and philosophical musings flourish in a generic environment that is about pushing the scientific boundaries of what is possible, while leaving plenty of room to ask the biggest questions about what it means to live and be human.

Bibliography

Abramovitch, Seth. 2013. "'Gravity' Spinoff: Watch the Other Side of Sandra Bullock's Distress Call (Exclusive Video)." *The Hollywood Reporter*, 20 November. Accessed April 14, 2021. https://www.hollywoodreporter.com/news/gravity-spinoff-watch-side-sandra-657919

Altman, Rick. 1984. "A Semantic/Syntactic Approach to Film Genre." *Cinema Journal* 23.3: 6–18.

Arnold-de Simine, Silke. 2019. "Beyond Trauma? Memories of Joi/y and Memory Play in *Blade Runner 2049*." *Memory Studies* 12.1: 61–73.

Arvan, Marcus. 2018. "Humans and Hosts in *Westworld*: What's the Difference?" In *Westworld and Philosophy: If You Go Looking for the Truth, Get the Whole Thing*, edited by James B. South and Kimberly S. Engels, 26–37. Hoboken, NJ: John Wiley and Sons, Inc.

Benwell, Bethan, and Stokoe, Elizabeth. 2006. *Discourse and Identity*. Edinburgh, Scotland: Edinburgh University Press.

Bishop, Brian. 2018. "Annihilation and Ex Machina Director Alex Garland on Using Sci-Fi to Explore Self-Destruction." *The Verge*, 21 February. Accessed January 29, 2021. https://www.theverge.com/2018/2/21/17029500/annihilation-ex-machina-director-alex-garland-sci-fi

Booker, M. Keith. 2001. *Monsters, Mushroom Clouds, and the Cold War: American Science Fiction and the Roots of Postmodernism, 1946–1964*. Westport, CT: Greenwood Press.

Boozer, Jack. 2008. "Introduction: The Screenplay and Authorship in Adaptation." In *Authorship in Film Adaptation*, edited by Jack Boozer, 1–30. Austin, TX: University of Texas Press.

Box Office Mojo. n.d.a. "2013 Worldwide Box Office." Accessed April 15, 2021. https://www.boxofficemojo.com/year/world/2013/?ref_=bo_cso_table_1

Box Office Mojo. n.d.b. "Arrival." *Box Office Mojo*. Accessed February 10, 2021. https://www.boxofficemojo.com/release/rl3195962881/

Box Office Mojo. n.d.c. "Contact." *Box Office Mojo.* Accessed February 10, 2021. https://www.boxofficemojo.com/release/rl3578430977/

Box Office Mojo. n.d.d. "Domestic Box Office For 2002." Accessed March 2, 2021. https://www.boxofficemojo.com/year/world/2002/?ref_=bo_cso_table_1

Busk, Larry Alan. 2016. "Westworld: Ideology, Simulation, Spectacle." *Mediations* 30.1: 25–38.

Brecht, Bertolt. 1964. *Brecht on Theatre: The Development of an Aesthetic.* Edited and translated by John Willett. New York: Hill and Wang.

Carroll, Noel. 1981. "Nightmare and the Horror Film: The Symbolic Biology of Fantastic Beings." *Film Quarterly* 34.3: 16–25.

Chapman, Andrew. 2012. "Privileging Form Over Content: Analysing Historical Videogames." *Journal of Digital Humanities* 1.2. Accessed June 30, 2015. http://journalofdigitalhumanities.org/1-2/privileging-form-over-content-by-adam-chapman/

Chiang, Ted. 2002. *Stories of Your Life and Others.* New York: Vintage Books.

Chitwood, Adam. 2017. "James Gray Says His Sci-Fi Movie 'Ad Astra' Starts Filming This Summer with Brad Pitt." *Collider*, 10 April. Accessed February 24, 2021. https://collider.com/james-gray-brad-pitt-ad-astra-filming/

Clarke, Arthur C. 2016. *2001: A Space Odyssey.* New York: Penguin Books.

Cohen, David S. 2016. "From Script to Screen: 'Eternal Sunshine Of The Spotless Mind.'" *Script*, 17 February. Accessed March 11, 2021. https://scriptmag.com/features/script-screen-eternal-sunshine-of-the-spotless-mind

Coontz, Stephanie. 1992. *The Way We Never Were: American Families and the Nostalgia Trap.* New York: Basic Books.

De Coster, Jori. 2011. "The Cyborg Villain: Mechanical Hybridity and Existential Fear." In *Villains: Global Perspectives on Villains and Villainy Today*, edited by Burcu Genc and Corinna Lenhardt, 219–228. Oxford: Inter-Disciplinary Press.

Deleuze, Gilles. 1993. *The Logic of Sense.* New York: Columbia University Press.

Delos Destinations. 2021. "About." *Delos Destinations.* Accessed March 25, 2021. https://www.delosdestinations.com/#about

Delos Destinations. 2021. "Experience." *Delos Destinations.* Accessed March 25, 2021. https://www.delosdestinations.com/#experience

Desser, David. 1997. "The New Eve: The Influence of *Paradise Lost* and *Frankenstein* on *Blade Runner.*" In *Retrofitting Blade Runner: Issues in Ridley Scott's* Blade Runner *and Philip K. Dick's* Do Androids Dream of Electric Sheep?, edited by Judith B. Kerman, 53–65. Madison, WI: The University of Wisconsin Press.

Dillon, Steven. 2006. *The Solaris Effect: Art and Artifice in Contemporary American Film.* Austin, TX: University of Texas Press.

Engle, John. 2016. "On Hopis and Heptapods: The Return of Sapir-Whorf." *ETC: A Review of General Semantics* 73.1: 95–99.

Engels, Kimberly S. 2018. "From William to the Man in Black: Sartrean Existentialism and the Power of Freedom." In *Westworld and Philosophy: If You Go Looking for the Truth, Get the Whole Thing*, edited by James B. South and Kimberly S. Engels, 125–135. Hoboken, NJ: John Wiley and Sons, Inc.

Falsetto, Mario. 2001. *Stanley Kubrick: A Narrative and Stylistic Analysis.* Westport, CT: Praeger Publishers.

Ferguson, Niall. 1999. "Virtual History: Towards a 'Chaotic' Theory of the Past." In *Virtual History: Alternatives and Counterfactuals,* edited by Niall Ferguson, 1–90. New York: Basic Books.

Fleming, David A., and Brown, William. 2018. "Through a (First) Contact Lens Darkly: *Arrival,* Unreal Time and Chthulucinema." *Film-Philosophy* 22.3: 340–363.

Fleming Jr., Mike. 2013. "Paramount, Scott Rudin Land 'Annihilation', First Installment Of Southern Reach Trilogy." *Deadline,* 26 March. Accessed February 1, 2021. https://deadline.com/2013/03/paramount-scott-rudin-land-annihilation-first-installment-of-southern-reach-trilogy-461655/

Flynn, Thomas. 2006. *Existentialism: A Very Short Introduction.* New York: Oxford University Press.

Frictional Games. 2021. "Press Kit." *Frictional Games.* Accessed March 23, 2021. https://frictionalgames.com/press-kit/

Frushtick, Russ. "Death Stranding review: Hideo Kojima Tries to Make Fetch Happen." *Polygon,* 1 November. Accessed April 6, 2021. https://www.polygon.com/reviews/2019/11/1/20942070/death-stranding-review-hideo-kojima-ps4

Fry, Carrol L. "From Technology to Transcendence: Humanity's Evolutionary Journey in *2001: A Space Odyssey.*" *Extrapolation* 44.3: 331–343.

Garland, Alex. 2018. "'Annihilation' Director Alex Garland Chats with CNET about the Upcoming Film." Interview by Connie Guglielmo. *CNET,* 8 February. Video, 31:48. Accessed on January 28, 2021. https://www.youtube.com/watch?v=nYhT5Ey42gg

Gauderault, André. 1987. "Theatricality, Narrativity, and Trickality: Reevaluating the Cinema of Georges Méliès." *Journal of Popular Film and Television* 15.3: 110–119.

Gault, Matthew. 2019. "'We're Not Thinking About Others.' What Hideo Kojima Wants You to Learn From Death Stranding." *Time,* 8 November. Accessed April 7, 2021. https://time.com/5722226/hideo-kojima-death-stranding/

Gray, Jonathan. 2010. *Show Sold Separately: Promos, Spoilers, and Other Media Paratexts.* New York: New York University Press.

Guynes, Sean. 2020. "Dystopia Fatigue Doesn't Cut It, or, *Blade Runner 2049*'s Utopian Longings." *Science Fiction Film and Television* 13.1: 143–148.

Gwaltney, Marilyn. 1997. "Androids as a Device for Reflection on Personhood." In *Retrofitting Blade Runner: Issues in Ridley Scott's* Blade Runner *and Philip K. Dick's* Do Androids Dream of Electric Sheep?, edited by Judith B. Kerman, 32–39. Madison, WI: The University of Wisconsin Press.

Hatfield, Daemon. 2011. "Limbo Review." *IGN,* 2 August. Accessed March 23, 2021. https://www.ign.com/articles/2011/08/02/limbo-review-2

Haugeland, John. 1997. "What is Mind Design?" In *Mind Design II: Philosophy, Psychology, Artificial Intelligence,* edited by John Haugeland, 1–28. Cambridge, MA: MIT Press.

Havens, Timothy, Lotz, Amanda D., and Tinic, Serra. 2009. "Critical Media Industry Studies: A Research Approach." *Communication, Culture & Critique* 2: 234–253.

Heinlein, Robert A. 2017. "On the Writing of Speculative Fiction." In *Science Fiction Criticism : An Anthology of Essential Writings*, edited by Rob Lantham, 17–21. New York: Bloomsbury Academic.

Hellekson, Karen. 2001. *The Alternative History: Refiguring Historical Time*. Kent, OH: Kent State University Press.

Heller-Nicholas, Alexandra. 2016. "Arrival (Denis Villeneuve, 2016)." *The Blue Lenses*. Accessed February 10, 2021. https://www.thebluelenses.com/post/154534849932/arrival-denis-villeneuve-2016-if-polytechnique

Hickman, Jonathan. 2019. *House of X #1*. New York. Marvel Comics.

Holden, Stephen. 2002. "FILM REVIEW; Their Love Will Go On In Outer Space." *The New York Times*, 27 November. Accessed March 3, 2021. https://www.nytimes.com/2002/11/27/movies/film-review-their-love-will-go-on-in-outer-space.html

Holloway, Daniel. 2017. "'Legion': Creator Noah Hawley on Taking FX Series Beyond X-Men." *Variety*, 24 January. Accessed on January 5, 2021 https://variety.com/2017/tv/news/legion-noah-hawley-fx-dan-stevens-1201967490/

James, Oliver, von Tunzelmann, Eugénie, Franklin, Paul, and Thorner, Kip S. 2015. "Gravitational Lensing by Spinning Black Holes in Astrophysics, and in the Movie Interstellar." *Classical and Quantum Gravity* 32: 1–41.

Jensen, Jeff. 2014. "Inside 'Interstellar,' Christopher Nolan's Emotional Space Odyssey." *Entertainment Weekly*, 16 October. Accessed February 10, 2021. https://ew.com/article/2014/10/16/interstellar-christopher-nolan-anne-hathaway/

Jordan, Miriam, and Haladyn, Julian Jason. 2010. "Simulation, Simulacra, and Solaris." *Film-Philosophy* 14.1: 253–273.

Juba, Joe. 2019. "Hideo Kojima Answers Our Questions About Death Stranding." *Game Informer*, 16 September. Accessed April 7, 2021. https://www.gameinformer.com/interview/2019/09/16/hideo-kojima-answers-our-questions-about-death-stranding

Karofsky, Amy, and Litch, Mary M. 2021. *Philosophy through Film*, 4th ed. New York: Routledge.

Kaylique, Zeb. 2019. "Blade Runner Dir. Ridley Scott (1982) Blade Runner 2049 Dir. Denis Villeneuve (2017)." *Existential Analysis: Journal of The Society for Existential Analysis* 30.1: 218–222.

Kit, Boris. 2017. "'Annihilation': Behind-the-Scenes of a Producer Clash and That Netflix Deal (Exclusive)." *The Hollywood Reporter*, 7 December. Accessed February 1, 2021. https://www.hollywoodreporter.com/heat-vision/annihilation-how-a-clash-between-producers-led-a-netflix-deal-1065465

Kojima, Hideo. n.d. "From Sapiens to Ludens." *Kojima Productions*. Accessed April 7, 2021. http://www.kojimaproductions.jp/en/#message

Lagerkvist Amanda. 2017. "Existential Media: Toward a Theorization of Digital Thrownness." *New Media & Society* 19.1: 96–110.

Lefebvre, Thierry. 2011. "*A Trip to the Moon*: A Composite Film." In *Fantastic Voyages of the Cinematic Imagination: Georges Méliès's* Trip to the Moon, edited by Matthew Solomon, 49–64. Albany, NY: SUNY Press.

Lem, Stanislaw. 2002. "The Solaris Station." *Stanislaw Lem - The Official Site,* 8 December. Accessed March 2, 2021. https://english.lem.pl/arround-lem/adaptations/solaris-soderbergh/147-the-solaris-station

Lizardi, Ryan. 2010. "'Re-Imagining' Hegemony and Misogyny in the Contemporary 'Slasher' Remake." *Journal of Popular Film and Television* 38.3: 113–121.

Lizardi. Ryan. 2013. "The Zombie Media Monster's Evolution to Empty Undead Signifier." In *Thinking Dead: What the Zombie Apocalypse Means*, edited by Murali Balaji, 89–104. Lanham, MD: Lexington Press.

Lizardi, Ryan. 2014a. "Bioshock: Complex and Alternate Histories." *Game Studies* 14.1. Accessed June 30, 2015. http://gamestudies.org/1401/articles/lizardi

Lizardi, Ryan. 2014b. *Mediated Nostalgia: Individual Memory and Contemporary Mass Media.* Lanham, MD: Lexington Press.

Luckhurst, Roger. 2017. *Science Fiction: A Literary History.* London: British Library Publishing.

Lycan, William G. 1996. *Consciousness and Experience.* Cambridge, MA: MIT Press.

Lyons, Siobhan. 2018. "Crossing the Uncanny Valley: What it Means to be Human in *Westworld.*" In *Westworld and Philosophy: If You Go Looking for the Truth, Get the Whole Thing*, edited by James B. South and Kimberly S. Engels, 41–49. Hoboken, NJ: John Wiley and Sons, Inc.

MacCabe, Colin. 2011. "Introduction: Bazinian Adaptation: *The Butcher Boy* as Example." In *True to the Spirit: Film Adaptation and the Question of Fidelity*, edited by Colin MacCabe, Kathleen Murray, and Rick Warner, 3–26. New York: Oxford University Press.

MacCallum-Stewart, E., & Parsler, J. 2007. "Controversies: Historicising the Computer Game." In *Situated Play, Proceedings of DiGRA 2007 Conference*, 203–10. Tokyo: The University of Tokyo.

Martín, Miguel Sebastián. 2018. "All the Park's a Stage: Westworld as the Metafictional *Frankenstein.*" *ES Review. Spanish Journal of English Studies* 39: 51–67.

McCarthy, Todd. 1997. "Contact." *Variety*, 7 July. Accessed February 10, 2021. https://variety.com/1997/film/reviews/contact-2-1117341257/

Merril, Judith. 2017. "What Do You Mean: Science? Fiction?" In *Science Fiction Criticism : An Anthology of Essential Writings*, edited by Rob Lantham, 22–36. New York: Bloomsbury Academic.

Mittel, Jason. 2015. *Complex TV: The Poetics of Contemporary Television Storytelling.* New York: New York University Press.

Morales-Campos, Arturo. 2016. "El Retorno a lo Humano en *Gravedad*, de Alfonso Cuarón." *La Colmena* 90: 9–21.

Morrissey, Thomas. 2004. "Growing Nowhere: Pinocchio Subverted in Spielberg's *A.I. Artificial Intelligence.*" *Extrapolation* 45.3: 249–262.

Netolicky, Deborah M. 2017. "Cyborgs, Desiring-Machines, Bodies Without Organs, and *Westworld*: Interrogating Academic Writing and Scholarly Identity." *KOME – An International Journal of Pure Communication Inquiry* 5.1: 91–103.

Newell, Catherine L. 2014. "The Greatest Adventure Awaiting Humankind: Destination Moon and Faith in the Future." *Implicit Religion* 17.4: 459–479.

North, Dale. 2015. "BioShock Franchise Sees Lifetime Sales of 25M Copies—With 11M from Infinite Alone." *Venture Beat*, June 1. Accessed June 30, 2015. http://venturebeat.com/2015/06/01/bioshock-franchise-sees-lifetime-sales-of-25m-copies-with-11m-from-infinite-alone/

Phinney, Jean S. "Identity Formation across Cultures: The Interaction of Personal, Societal, and Historical Change." *Human Development* 43: 27–31.

Powers, Korine. "Playing Pregnant in Death Stranding." Presentation at the annual conference of the Electronic Literature Organization, Virtual, July 16–19. Accessed April 6, 2021. https://stars.library.ucf.edu/elo2020/asynchronous/talks/19/

Purse, Lisa. 2017. "Working Space: *Gravity* (Alfonso Cuarón) and the Digital Long Take." In *The Long Take: Critical Approaches*, edited by J. Gibbs and D. Pye, 221–238. London: Palgrave Macmillan.

Radiohead. 1994. "Fake Plastic Trees." Track #4 on *The Bends*. Parlophone, 1995. CD.

Radiohead. 1997. "Exit Music (For a Film)." Track #4 on *OK Computer*. Parlophone and Capitol Records. CD.

Roberts, Adam. 2016. *The History of Science Fiction*. London: Palgrave Macmillan.

Rose, Steve. 2014. "Sandra Bullock: the Pain of Gravity." *The Guardian*, 6 February. Accessed February 16, 2021. https://www.theguardian.com/film/2014/feb/06/sandra-bullock-pain-gravity-oscars-george-clooney-2014

Rosenberg, Alyssa. 2014. "Opinion: How Ken Burns' Surprise Role in 'Interstellar' Explains the Movie." *The Washington Post*, 6 November. Accessed February 9, 2021. https://www.washingtonpost.com/news/act-four/wp/2014/11/06/how-ken-burns-surprise-role-in-interstellar-explains-the-movie/

Rosenstone, Robert A. 1995. *Visions of the Past: The Challenge of Film to Our Idea of History*. Cambridge, MA: Harvard University Press.

Rothman, Joshua. 2015. "The Weird Thoreau." *The New Yorker*, 14 January. https://www.newyorker.com/culture/cultural-comment/weird-thoreau-jeff-vandermeer-southern-reach

Sandner, David. 1998. "Shooting for the Moon: Méliès, Verne, Wells, and the Imperial Satire." *Extrapolation* 39.1: 5–25.

Sartre, Jean-Paul. 2007. *Existentialism is a Humanism*. New Haven, CT: Yale University Press.

Schauer, Bradley. 2015. "'The Greatest Exploitation Special Ever': *Destination Moon* and Postwar Independent Distribution." *Film History* 27.1: 1–28.

Schauer, Bradley. 2016. *Escape Velocity: American Science Fiction Film, 1950–1982*. Middletown CT: Wesleyan University Press.

Scholes, Robert, and Rabkin, Eric S. 1977. *Science Fiction: History, Science, Vision*. Oxford: Oxford University Press.

Schrader, Benjamin. 2019. "Cyborgian Self-Awareness: Trauma and Memory in *Blade Runner* and *Westworld*." *Theory and Event* 22.4: 820–841.

Searle, John R. 1980. "Minds, Brains, and Programs." *The Behavioral and Brain Sciences* 3: 417–457.

Sobchack, Vivian. 1997. *Screening Space: The American Science Fiction Film*, 2nd ed. New Brunswick, NJ: Rutgers University Press.

South, James B., and Engels, Kimberly S, editors. 2018. *Westworld and Philosophy: If You Go Looking for the Truth, Get the Whole Thing*. Hoboken, NJ: John Wiley and Sons, Inc.

Stam, Robert. 2000. "Beyond Fidelity: The Dialogics of Adaptation." In *Film Adaptation*, edited by James Naremore, 54–76. New Brunswick, NJ: Rutgers University Press.

Steiman, Harvey. 2014. "Terroir? What Exactly Do You Mean?" *Wine Spectator*, 7 April. Accessed February 3, 2014. https://www.winespectator.com/articles/terroir-what-exactly-do-you-mean-49735

Smeekes, Anouk, and Verkuyten, Maykel. 2015. "The Presence of the Past: Identity Continuity and Group Dynamics." *European Review of Social Psychology* 26.1: 162–202.

Tani, Shotaro, and Natti, Yuji. 2017. "Gaming 'God' Hideo Kojima Has a Vision for Us Homo Sapiens." *Nikkei Asia*, 9 February. Accessed April 6, 2021. https://asia.nikkei.com/Business/Gaming-god-Hideo-Kojima-has-a-vision-for-us-Homo-sapiens

Telotte, J.P. 2001. *Science Fiction Film*. Edinburgh, UK: Cambridge University Press.

Thiess, Derek. 2014. *Relativism, Alternate History, and the Forgetful Reader: Reading Science Fiction and Historiography*. New York: Lexington Books.

Thorne, Kip. 2014. *The Science of Interstellar*. New York: W.W. Norton and Company.

Tompkins, David. 2014. "Weird Ecology: On The Southern Reach Trilogy." *Los Angeles Review of Books*, 30 September. Accessed February 4, 2021. https://lareviewofbooks.org/article/weird-ecology-southern-reach-trilogy

Trushell, John M. 2004. "American Dreams of Mutants: The X-Men 'Pulp' Fiction, Science Fiction, and Superheroes." *Journal of Popular Culture* 38.1: 49–168.

Tumanov, Vladimir. 2016. "Philosophy of Mind and Body in Andrei Tarkovsky's *Solaris*." *Film-Philosophy* 20: 357–375.

Turing, A.M. 1997. "Computing Machinery and Intelligence." In *Mind Design II: Philosophy, Psychology, Artificial Intelligence*, edited by John Haugeland, 29–56. Cambridge, MA: MIT Press.

Uricchio, W. 2005. "Simulation, History, and Computer Games." In *Handbook of Computer Game Studies,* edited by Joost Raessens and Jeffrey H. Goldstein, 327–38. Cambridge: MIT Press.

Vandermeer, Jeff. 2014. *Area X: The Southern Reach Trilogy: Annihilation; Authority; Acceptance*. New York: Farrar, Straus and Giroux.

Verevis, Constantine. 2017. "Remakes, Sequels, Prequels." In *The Oxford Handbook of Adaptation Studies*, edited by Thomas Leitch, 267–284. New York: Oxford University Press.

Versteeg, Michael, and Brakman, Adam. 2018. "Does the Piano Play Itself? Consciousness and the Eliminativism of Robert Ford." In *Westworld and Philosophy: If You Go Looking for the Truth, Get the Whole Thing*, edited by James B. South and Kimberly S. Engels, 90–101. Hoboken, NJ: John Wiley and Sons, Inc.

Vineyard, Jennifer. 2016a. "How Music Is Controlling the Hosts on *Westworld*." *Vulture*, 23 November. Accessed March 24, 2021. https://www.vulture.com/2016/11/westworld-how-music-is-controlling-the-hosts.html

Vineyard, Jennifer. 2016b. "How Radiohead's 'Exit Music (for a Film)' Reflects Dolores's Climactic Westworld Moment." *Vulture*, 6 December. Accessed March 24, 2021. https://www.vulture.com/2016/12/westworld-radiohead-dolores-finale.html

Weinstock, Jeffrey Andrew. 2014. "American Monsters." In *A Companion to American Gothic*, edited by Charles L. Crow, 41–55. Malden, MA: John Wiley and Sons, Ltd.

Wigler, Josh. 2019. "'Legion' Series Finale: Noah Hawley Explains the Time-Bending Ending." *The Hollywood Reporter*, 12 August. Accessed on January 15, 2021. https://www.hollywoodreporter.com/live-feed/legion-series-finale-explained-noah-hawley-ending-1230904

Wilson, Janelle. 2005. *Nostalgia: Sanctuary of Meaning*. Lewisburg, PA: Bucknell University Press.

Winckler, Reto. 2017. "This Great Stage of Androids: *Westworld*, Shakespeare and the World as Stage." *Journal of Adaptation in Film & Performance* 10.2: 169–188.

Woerner, Meredith. 2013. "Gravity's Ending Holds a Deeper Meaning, says Alfonso Cuarón." *Gizmodo*, 8 October. Accessed February 16, 2021. https://io9.gizmodo.com/gravitys-ending-holds-a-deeper-meaning-says-alfonso-c-1442690788

Wood, David. 2001. "Invasion of the Body Snatchers (1956)." *BBC*, 1 May. Accessed March 8, 2021. http://www.bbc.co.uk/films/2001/05/01/invasion_of_the_body_snatchers_1956_review.shtml

Zeitchik, Steven. 2016. "Decoding the Linguistic Geekiness Behind 'Arrival's' Sci-Fi Sheen." *Los Angeles Times*, 25 November. Accessed January 25, 2021. https://www.latimes.com/entertainment/movies/la-et-mn-arrival-movie-linguist-20161125-story.html

Index

2001: A Space Odyssey, 17–20
adaptations, 64–65, 69, 77
Ad Astra, 21, 40–47
A.I.: Artificial Intelligence, 28–30
Alien franchise, 16, 31; *Alien: Covenant*, 32. See also *Prometheus*
allegory, 12–13
alternative history, 112–13
android, 16, 24–25, 28–29, 31–32, 93–101, 103–6, 108–10
Annihilation: book, 65–68; film, 68–74; Southern Reach trilogy, 74–75
antagonist, viii–ix, 11, 18, 22, 36–37, 40, 49–50, 54, 111, 130, 135, 144–45
apocryphal history, 122, 124, 126. See also alternative history
Arrival, ix, 55–61
Assassin's Creed series, 121–26

Bioshock series, 113–21
black hole, 50, 53–55
Black Mirror, 136
Blade Runner, 23–26
Blade Runner 2049, 26–27
Brecht, Bertolt, 130

Carroll, Noel. See overreacher plot
consciousness, 21, 46, 82, 84, 86–88, 101–3, 107, 132–38
Contact, ix–x, 56

counterfactual history, 112–13, 115, 122. See also alternative history
Cuarón, Alfonso, 38–40. See also *Gravity*

Death Stranding, 138–41
Destination Moon, 8–9
Dick, Philip K., 23, 132

Earth vs. the Flying Saucers, 11
eliminativism, 107–8
Eternal Sunshine of the Spotless Mind, 30
existence, viii, 17, 24, 26–27, 29–30, 37–38, 41, 47, 62, 80, 86, 91, 106–7
existentialism, viii–ix, 22, 25–26, 37–38, 44, 46, 80, 89, 106, 111, 129–30; atheistic, 38, 41
Ex Machina, ix, 76

Flash Gordon, 6–7
The Fly, 12
Flynn, Thomas, 38, 50, 53, 60, 74, 80, 89
Frankenstein, 6
Futureworld, 96–97

Garland, Alex, 64, 69, 73, 76. See also *Annihilation*, movie
generations, 39–40, 45, 47, 52

Index

Gravity, 35–40

Heidegger, Martin, 130

identity, xi, 49, 55, 62, 72, 75, 81, 84, 86, 88–89, 91, 132
interactivity, 111, 115, 124–25, 129–33, 137–39
Interstellar, ix, 50–55

King of the Rocketmen, 7
Kojima, Hideo, 138–41. *See also Death Stranding*
Kubrick, Stanley, 19, 28. *See also 2001: A Space Odyssey*; *A.I.: Artificial Intelligence*

Lagerkvist, Amanda, 80, 111, 129–30, 142
Legion, 79–92
Lem, Stanislaw, 20–21. *See also Solaris*
Limbo, 131
linguistics, 57–58; Sapir-Whorf hypothesis, 59

The Martian, ix, 37
Méliès, George. *See A Trip to the Moon*
memory, 21, 23, 26–27, 30, 56–57, 60, 62, 85, 107, 121, 125
Metropolis, 5–6

Nolan, Christopher. *See Interstellar*

nostalgia, 87–88, 138, 141

overreacher plot, 11–12

paratexts, 77
Prometheus, 30–32

remakes, 22, 93–94

Sartre, Jean-Paul, 38, 41, 46, 106. *See also* existentialism
Schauer, Bradley, 2–3, 7–8
science fiction: genre, 2, 3, 7–10, 15–16, 19, 22, 24, 49, 80–81, 111–12, 138, 141, 144–46; literature, 1–2, 112; semantic/syntactic, 2, 8
Shelley, Mary. *See Frankenstein*
Solaris, 20–23
SOMA, 131–38
Spielberg, Steven, 28
The Stanley Parable, 131
Stories of Your Life, 56, 61

Them!, 10–11
A Trip to the Moon, 4–5

Westworld film, 93–96
Westworld television series, 97–110
wormhole, 52

X-Men, 79–81, 83. *See also Legion*

About the Author

Ryan Lizardi is associate professor of digital media and humanities at SUNY Polytechnic Institute. He focuses his research on media encouraged nostalgia, including his books *Mediated Nostalgia* (2014), *Nostalgic Generations and Media* (2017), and *Subjective Experiences of Interactive Nostalgia* (editor, 2019); explorations of television remakes; and science fiction media.